This book belongs to

....

Cooking with Flowers

Sweet and Savory Recipes with Rose Petals, Lilacs,
Lavender, and Other Edible Flowers

by Miche Bacher of Mali B Sweets

photography by Miana Jun

QUIRK BOOKS

PHILADELPHIA

This is for my boys—your Mama loves you. You will always be the most favorite flowers in my garden.

Library of Congress Cataloging in Publication Number:
    2012936106

ISBN: 978-1-59474-625-3
Printed in China
Typeset in Aire, Adobe Caslon, and Trade Gothic
Designed by Katie Hatz
Photography by Miana Jun
Additional photography by Miche Bacher: inside back cover
    (portraits); Jenny Gorman: jacket flap (author's portrait);
    and Anthony LaScala: jacket flap (photographer's portrait).
    All used by permission of the photographers.
    Prop styling by Miche Bacher, Miana Jun,
    Nanao Anton, Kristine Trevino, and Anthony LaScala
Production management by John J. McGurk

Quirk Books
215 Church St.
Philadelphia, PA 19106
quirkbooks.com
10 9 8 7 6 5 4 3 2 1

Disclaimer:
Eat flowers only when you're sure they're edible and
organically grown. When trying new edible flowers, introduce
them to your diet in small quantities and beware of allergies.
No book should be a substitute for a reader's good judgment
and common sense.

Contents

Introduction

I set out to fill this book with my favorite recipes for edible flowers. I love to cook with beauties like roses and orchids; humble potted plants like pansies and geraniums; herb flowers like chamomile, rosemary, and sage blossoms; and wild weed flowers like dandelions and violets. Some of these flowers relish their time in the cold, such as elder, and some of them thrive in the tropics, like hibiscus. You'll find that each recipe is designed to make use of a particular bloom, but I will show you how to swap blossoms when appropriate.

To give you some background information, each chapter opens with a piece about the flower, including its botanical name, nicknames, growing habits and seasonality, culinary uses, and anything special you might need to know to prepare it before cooking with it. You'll also find each flower's meaning according to the Victorian language of flowers, plus some fascinating bits of history and legend. The back of the book is filled with a collection of basic yet flavorful recipes—simple classics you can make with almost any edible flower. Stock up on these, and you'll have a flower-filled kitchen all year long.

Why Eat Flowers?

What's that you say? Eat your flowers?
It's true. There are lots of flowers you can eat. Taking the time to learn which ones are edible and how to enjoy them is well worth the effort. I have been eating flowers for years and take pleasure in introducing them to others.

Flowers add color, complexity, and what I like to call the magical "what's in it" factor to your food. They are full of nutrients and often offer health benefits, too. You don't have to be a master gardener or trained chef to cook with flowers—once you start looking, you'll realize edible blossoms are all around you, and it really is a breeze to use them. Soon you'll find yourself searching farmers' market and neighborhood gardens for both cultivated flowers and what some might call weeds.

Have *I* ever eaten one?
Many people have eaten flowers without even realizing it. If you've ever had zucchini blossoms, you have eaten a flower. Artichoke? Flower. Brussels spouts? Flower. Broccoli, cauliflower? Flower, flower. Although those are all fabulous flowers in their own right, in this book we'll focus on the widely available types that don't get the culinary attention they deserve.

What do flowers taste like?
Chive blossoms and nasturtiums are spicy, sunflowers are bitter, and calendula and chamomile are earthy. Lilacs can be highly perfumed, and their taste varies from slightly bitter to lemony. Roses can be sweet, with back notes of spice or mint or apple; the stronger the scent, the more pronounced the flavor. Geranium flavors vary wildly, from lime to rose to orange to mint and more. But most flowers have a fairly consistent flavor that varies subtly due to the cultivar, soil type, and growing conditions.

Don't be afraid to switch it up and try different flowers in different recipes. If you find a flower you love, try substituting it for one you're not quite fond of. Lavender is the only flower you have to be cautious with, because its flavor and aroma can be overwhelming, so start by using a lot less lavender than you think you'll need. I can still hear my father's voice echoing in my ear: "You can always add, but you can't take out." And he could cook!

Are flowers good for you?
For centuries, flowers have been prized for their medicinal and cosmetic properties. Flowers have been found in Egyptian tombs. Ancient Romans used mallows, pinks, and roses. Chrysanthemums, daylilies, and orchids have long been beloved across Asia. Today, we use flower remedies in acupuncture and herbal medicine—chamomile to soothe stomachaches and relax the nerves, lavender for depression, violets for coughs. Many flowers are high in vitamins and minerals like vitamins A and C, and they are all low in calories. The Memorial Sloan-Kettering Cancer Center website provides information on herbs and flowers that may be useful in cancer treatment. It's exciting to see modern medical research into each blossom's nutritional benefits and healing properties.

Flowers have also found their places in legends and myths about healing (and breaking!) relationships. Because I love a good story, I can't wait to share some of them with you, such as how the pansy got its name (page 128) and how Vishna and Brahma's argument over the rose was solved (page 136).

What is the language of flowers?
Victorians cherished recipes for flower teas, cakes, and salads as well as gem-colored flower jellies, jams, and conserves. They also used flowers as a means of communication. That's how the legendary language of flowers evolved: people would send each other single flowers, bouquets, and "tussie-mussies" (small symmetrical bouquets) as a means of private and highly nuanced communication. Each flower conveyed a sentiment, and sometimes different colors of flowers conveyed different meanings. So if you received a coral rose you might be the subject of desire, but if you were given a lavender one you might have enchanted someone.

From Garden to Table

So, are there rules about eating flowers? In a couple words: you betcha! When grown organically, flowers like roses, lilacs, and little herb blossoms are full of flavor, color, and nutrients. But whether you're buying them in a store or gathering them yourself, you must use your best judgment and follow these basic rules.

Gathering Flowers

Know your flowers. Not all flowers are edible, and some are poisonous. Arm yourself with a reputable plant guide, such as Peterson's *Field Guide to Edible Wild Plants*, or read the online plant database of Cornell University (gardening. cornell.edu/homegardening).

Select only flowers that have been grown organically, whether they're from the farmers' market, an organic grocery store, or your own garden. Commercial florist flowers have been sprayed with chemicals you don't want to eat, so avoid any bouquets and single stems for sale in the supermarket or florist shop unless they are labeled USDA organic for culinary use.

Foraging for flowers can be rewarding, but **avoid anything growing by the road.** Plants can absorb all the toxins from car exhaust and other auto-related emissions. Be sure you have properly identified all foraged flowers before consuming them (see plant guide information, above).

Use caution if you have hayfever, asthma, or allergies, because you may be more likely to have a flower allergy as well. As with any new food, start slowly and introduce flowers into your diet a little at a time.

Ready the flowers for kitchen use. Always clean and "debuggify" flowers before cooking with them.

Readying Flowers

Preparing flowers for culinary use is similar to preparing herbs, fruits, and vegetables. Here's how:

1. **Pick edible flowers in the morning,** when they're fresh with new blossoms that have opened with the first rays of the sun. Choose them as you would most produce, plucking clean healthy-looking flowers in their prime and avoiding older bruised blossoms. Taste them before using them in a recipe.

2. **Store them well.** If you are not going to use your flowers right away, there are several things you can do. Long-stemmed flowers can be placed in water for a day or two before cooking. Others can be stored between lay-ers of paper towels in the fridge. (I find the maximum length of time I can keep flowers in an airtight container in the refrigerator is just shy of one week.) Some short-stemmed flowers (like borage) are so delicate you can't store them, so they're best used right away.

3. **Wash them!** Rinse flowers gently and thoroughly with lots of water. Pat dry. Some flowers, like dandelions, are great hiding places for more than a few insects and may need a slightly stronger solution. In the case of persistent bugs, a quick swish in salt water is enough to do the trick.

4. **Prep as necessary.** Each flower has its own preparation needs, but generally speaking you will want to remove the stamens, styles, pistils, and sepals, which are the

stalks that hold the pollen and the green stem that holds the petals together (basically, everything but the petals). For flowers like lilies and hibiscus, a little pollen might fall off the stamens and require some brushing off. See each flower's preparation notes at the beginning of each chapter for specific instructions.

5. **Experiment.** Many edible flowers are interchangeable, so once you find ones you love to eat, you can try them in most any recipe in this book. It's typically an equal substitution, unless you're using lavender flowers; these are particularly potent, so too much can overpower any dish. Just reduce the amount of lavender and do the occasional taste test when trying it in new flower recipes.

Measuring Flowers

All flower measurements are approximate because measuring flowers is an art, not a science. Flowers come in so many different sizes, you can't (and don't need to) measure perfectly precise numbers of blossoms per cup. Think of flowers like herbs and spices: it's hard to overdo it as long as you stay somewhat close to the general measurement and taste test as you cook.

Selecting Ingredients

Quality ingredients will let the flavors of your flowers shine.

Flour: All-purpose flour is the flour of choice unless otherwise noted. At Mali B, we like the quality of Bob's Red Mill, but many excellent and affordable types are available.

Eggs: Use large eggs unless otherwise indicated. We recommend choosing organic eggs—local, free-range—whenever possible. The yolks are deep yellow and the taste is unsurpassed. Show your local chickens some love!

Butter: All recipes in this book call for unsalted European butter, which is higher in fat content, because we love its fresh, creamy taste. If you don't use this type of butter, you may want to add a smidge more butter here and there to compensate.

Sugar: Always use granulated sugar unless otherwise indicated. We swear by organic granulated cane sugar; we think it keeps our sweets less sweet.

Calendulas

Botanical Name: *Calendula*

Nicknames: Pot marigold, poor man's saffron

Language of Flowers: Calendulas signify sacred affections, joy, grief, and remembrance.

Background: Legend has it that calendula blooms almost every month, earning it the name *kalendae*. Its common name (marigold) honors the Virgin Mary, who wore a calendula flower. For all the loveliness and joy the calendula symbolizes, it also represents a bit of anguish. In Wales, the plant is thought to induce a weakness for drunkenness if looked upon, let alone picked. In Mexico, it is a symbol for the Day of the Dead; some say that the flower rose from the blood of natives massacred by Spanish invaders.

Culinary Use: Calendula is spicy and peppery. Because it imparts a golden color, it is known as the "poor man's saffron" and is used for tinting custards, eggs, and rice dishes. Farmers feed calendula to their hens in an effort to deepen the color of the yolks in their eggs.

Seasonality: In many climates, calendula grows year-round. In most of North America, it is available from late spring through early autumn. Calendula plants begin appearing in garden centers and nurseries in early spring. Be sure not to confuse calendulas with tagetes, which are also known as marigolds. Calendula looks daisy-like and has curved seeds, whereas tagetes resembles a pom-pom with short, thick petals and long, dark seeds. I like to plant my calendula near my tomatoes and asparagus because they deter the pests that like to feast on those tender vegetables. (As a bonus, calendula butter over steamed asparagus is pretty flavorful, and calendula petals brighten up a plate of tomato salad.)

Preparation: Pick calendula flowers at the base of their heads. Give them a good wash and a spin through a salad spinner. Pat dry. Next, clutch a small cluster of the petals and pull to release them from their centers.

Measure: 1 cup calendula petals = petals from about 40 to 60 flowers.

Calendula Cornbread

My friend Susan's cornbread is the best I've ever tasted, so I'm thankful she let me share a flower-filled version of her recipe here. It's moist and tender, a cross between pudding and cornbread (for a firmer cornbread, use slightly less cream corn). Susan's secret is the cream corn—mine is the calendula. It brings an even deeper golden hue and a peppery taste to this delicious dish. *Makes one 9-inch skillet.*

1. Preheat oven to 400°F. Place butter in a 9-inch skillet and set it in the oven for a moment to melt. Swirl melted butter to coat the bottom of the pan.

2. Mix together cornmeal, flour, calendula petals, baking soda, baking powder, and salt in a medium bowl. Make a well in the center for egg and buttermilk, drop them in, and stir until just combined. Stir in cream corn.

3. Pour half the batter into the skillet. Top with about ¾ cup of the cheese, reserving the rest to make a crunchy cheesy topping that you won't regret. Arrange a layer of onion, chilies, and jalapeño (if using) on top. Cover with the rest of the batter and then sprinkle with the rest of the cheese. Bake for about 20 minutes, or until lightly browned.

Cornbread for a Crowd

You can double this recipe and bake it in a 12-inch skillet. Double everything but about half of the second can of cream corn and the second egg for firmer cornbread.

Calendula used to be called "poor man's saffron" and was used to give cheese its yellow-orange color before the days of chemical colorings. So anytime you see saffron in a recipe, remember that you can reach into your garden for a bit of calendula instead.

1 tablespoon unsalted butter
1 cup stone-ground cornmeal*
⅓ cup all-purpose flour
½ cup calendula petals (from about 20 flowers)
¼ teaspoon baking soda
1 teaspoon baking powder
1 teaspoon salt
1 egg, beaten
1 cup buttermilk
1 (14¾-ounce) can cream corn
1 cup (4 ounces) Manchego cheese,** grated and divided
1 small yellow onion, diced
1 (4-ounce) can chopped green chilies (optional)
1 fresh jalapeño, chopped (optional)

*I like this cornmeal for its coarse texture. When it's ground, the hull and kernel are left in the mix, giving the meal a deeper corn taste. It's also more perishable, so find a spot in your freezer to store leftovers.

**Cheddar or just about any hard cheese will do.

Calendula Quiche

I hope you can forgive me if I was misleading. This is indeed a quiche, but it's a crustless one. If you love crust, don't do without it; pour the egg custard into a prebaked pie crust and then bake as directed below. Calendula blends so well into eggs and cheese that you'll wonder why you ever made eggs without it. *Makes one 9-inch quiche.*

3 cups loosely packed fresh spinach
1 tablespoon extra-virgin olive oil
4 eggs
1 cup heavy cream
¾ cup (6 ounces) soft goat cheese, crumbled
½ cup calendula petals (from about 20 flowers)
½ teaspoon salt

1. Preheat oven to 375°F. Liberally butter a 9-inch pie pan.

2. In a skillet over medium heat, cook spinach in olive oil until the leaves are fully wilted, about 3 minutes. Drain.

3. Whisk eggs and cream together. Add goat cheese, calendula petals, and salt and whisk again.

4. Arrange spinach in the bottom of the prepared pie plate and pour egg mixture over top. Bake for about 25 minutes, or until the custard is set in the center and the top is golden brown.

Calendula Scrambled Eggs

Calendula is a happy complement to any egg dish, and this one couldn't be easier. Use about 2 flowers' worth of petals (or 2 tablespoons chopped petals) per egg. Whisk them in with a sprinkle of salt and pepper while you're breaking up the eggs.

Daylilies and other flowers also work well with eggs. Serve flower quiches, flower scrambled eggs—even flower omelets—for breakfast.

Calendula Ravioli

Putting herbs in pasta dough is not new, but little calendula flecks are a welcome addition. Filling the dough with garden-fresh herbs, earthy goat cheese, and bittersweet calendula lets the natural buttery flavor of the flower take center stage. *Makes about 40 ravioli; serves 4 to 6.*

1. Put flours, salt, eggs, oil, and calendula petals in the bowl of a mixer fitted with a dough hook. Mix on medium-low speed just until a ball forms.

   Many people combine dough by hand, others use a food processor, and some prefer a mixer. Whatever works for you is fine. I like the mixer because the food processor beats up my dough a little too much, and I often don't have the time to fully knead by hand.

2. Turn the dough onto a work surface dusted with flour. Knead for 3 minutes until it feels smooth and elastic. Cover kneaded dough in plastic wrap and let it rest for about 30 minutes. This is the perfect time to make the filling, if you haven't already.

3. Line a baking sheet with parchment paper and lightly dust a work surface with flour. Divide the dough in half or thirds. Working with one portion at a time (and keeping the other portions covered so they don't dry out), roll dough until it is thin and narrow enough to pass through your pasta machine. Roll it through the machine until it's about $1/16$ inch thick. Place that piece on the floured work surface. Cut rolled dough into 2-inch strips, fill half the strips with scant tablespoons of filling about 2 inches apart, and reserve the other half for the tops.

   Pasta rolling can be a team sport, with one person cranking and the other guiding the dough.

4. Dip your finger in water and run it around the border of each ravioli. Place the top strips of pasta over the bottoms and gently press the edges to seal. Try to "burp" the dough to remove air pockets. Cut ravioli strips into 2-inch squares. Dust the tops with semolina and place ravioli on the prepared baking sheet. Repeat with the rest of the dough. You can set the pasta aside for up to 2 hours at room temperature or you can cook it immediately. It's best when fresh.

2½ cups all-purpose flour, plus more for dusting
½ cup semolina flour*
1 teaspoon salt
4 eggs, lightly beaten, plus 1 more
1 tablespoon extra-virgin olive oil
¼ cup calendula petals (from about 12 flowers)
2 cups filling (page 16)

OPTIONAL TOPPINGS
About 6 tablespoons butter
3 cloves garlic, minced
Splash white wine

*Semolina flour comes from durum wheat and is high in gluten, which makes for a nice elastic dough. It is also higher in protein and fiber and lower in sugars than all-purpose flour. Most important, it gives pasta a fuller, richer flavor. If you can't find it, use all-purpose instead.

You can also freeze ravioli overnight by arranging them in a single layer on baking sheets lined with parchment paper (note that the pasta will take on a gray cast if left overnight in the fridge; there is no avoiding this). Pop the frozen ravioli into freezer bags for cooking later.

5. To cook, bring a large pot of lightly salted water to a boil. Gently drop in enough ravioli to make a single layer in the pot (usually 6 to 8 pieces) and cook for 5 minutes, or until they are cooked through but still have bite. Use a slotted spoon to move them onto serving plates. I don't think calendula ravioli need more than a bit of melted butter, a hint of garlic, and a splash of white wine, but, by all means, use the topping of your choice.

Herbed Goat Cheese and Calendula Ravioli Filling

1 cup (8 ounces) soft goat cheese
⅓ cup (2 ounces) finely grated Parmesan cheese
¼ cup (4 ounces) ricotta cheese
2 tablespoons chopped calendula petals (from about 4 flowers)
1 tablespoon chopped fresh herbs, such as parsley, basil, and chives, or whatever you have on hand

Crab and Calendula Ravioli Filling

1 cup lump crabmeat
¾ cup ricotta cheese
1 shallot, minced
2 tablespoons chopped calendula petals (from about 4 flowers)
1 teaspoon finely minced parsley
Pinch salt

The ingredients are different, but the method for making these ravioli fillings is the same. Toss all ingredients together in a bowl. Cover and refrigerate until you are ready to use. The crab version in particular is a make-and-use filling; you won't want to store it for more than a few hours. Makes about 2 cups.

Flower Ravioli

If you love the flavor of calendula ravioli, why not try making the pasta with other flowers? Herb flowers, sunflowers, dandelions, and nasturtiums are all excellent choices. Experimenting with swapping in one or several other flowers is a good way to extend your flower-ravioli season.

Calendula Orange Cake

I have been making celebration cakes for as long as I can remember. I love the way a frosted layer cake makes any occasion feel more like a party. My favorite frosted cakes are simple and look so good you want to dive into them. This calendula cake is exactly that. Slathered with a cream cheese frosting—which you just might be tempted to eat by itself—it looks scrumptious on the outside and tastes delicious on the inside. *Makes three 8-inch round layers, or 1 layer cake.*

1. Preheat oven to 325°F. Line the bottoms of three 8-inch round cake pans with parchment paper and coat them with nonstick spray.

2. Whir sugar and zest in a food processor for 2 to 30 seconds, or until it releases a sweet orange aroma.

3. Sift flour, baking soda, and salt together in a bowl. In the bowl of a mixer, beat butter and orange sugar on medium speed for 5 minutes, or until light and fluffy.

   Don't skimp on sifting. It really does matter, especially for cakes and other tender baked goods. Flour gets compacted while sitting in the container waiting for you to use it, so it needs a bit of fluffing before measuring. If you don't sift, the same volume of flour will weigh a lot more and cause your cake to be heavier and denser.

4. Beat in eggs one at a time, scraping the sides of the bowl so the mixture is smooth. Reduce speed to low and add half the flour mixture; then mix in yogurt and orange juice. Beat in the remaining flour mixture and calendula petals.

5. Distribute batter among the pans and bake for about 50 minutes, or until a metal tester comes out clean. Let cakes cool to room temperature in pans and then turn them out and flip them upright. Let them cool for at least 1 hour and up to overnight; after an hour, tightly cover each layer in plastic wrap and store at room temperature until ready to frost.

6. Mark the lowest spot in the top of the first cake layer. With a serrated knife, use a slow sawing motion and circle around the cake, cutting off the uneven

3 cups sugar

Zest and juice of 1 orange

4½ cups cake flour

1 teaspoon baking soda

¾ teaspoon salt

1½ cups (3 sticks) unsalted butter, room temperature

9 eggs

1½ cups full-fat Greek yogurt

½ cup calendula petals (from about 25 flowers),* plus extra to decorate

8 cups (1 batch) calendula flower frosting (page 183)

*Use petals of a single color or try any mix of colors that you like.

top. (Good news is, you can sample this yummy crusty piece.) Repeat with remaining layers.

7. Place the first layer cut-side down on your serving dish. Spread frosting on top with an offset spatula or a good flexible spatula. Top with another upside-down layer of cake and repeat the process twice more. Frost the outside of the cake with the remaining frosting.

You might consider applying a "crumb coat": put on only a light layer of frosting (just to seal any crumbs), refrigerate the cake for about a half hour to give the frosting some time to solidify, and then take it out and finish frosting it.

8. Time to decorate. Try using calendula petals in different colors as confetti. Toss them onto the cake, sprinkle them down like rain, shower them like asteroids—you are the artist, and you can't go wrong.

To build a cake: First you tort. Next you fill. Then you frost. Finally you decorate. Torting is the process of leveling each layer so that you don't end up with a leaning (or tumbling) tower of cake.

Flowerfetti Cake

At our confectionery shop, Mali B, Nanao and I are often asked to make Funfetti cakes. Something about the sprinkles inside and the festive colors makes people feel young. But I think flower petals are the original cake confetti. Colorful, flavorful, textural, flower petals. They're irresistible when it comes time to bring a frosted cake to a summer party.

Make the cake recipe on page 18 but swap in the zest and juice of 3 small lemons for the orange zest and juice. Substitute an array of flower petals—whatever is fresh and growing—for the calendula. I like roses, dianthus, bachelor buttons, and marigold.

Calendula Cookies

Sugar and spice and everything nice is what these cookies are made of. Take a bite through the crisp and airy exterior of this unassuming little cookie and into the softer inside full of sweet and spicy ginger, tangy lemon, and earthy calendula. You'll never look at a plain sugar cookie again. *Makes 24 cookies.*

1. Preheat oven to 350°F. Line 2 baking sheets with parchment paper.

2. Pulse sugar and zest in a food processor until fully combined, with the zest releasing its volatile oils. The whole room will fill with the aroma of lemon in about 5 good pulses, or about 30 seconds, when the sugar captures all the fragrance the lemon releases. I find this extra step makes my cookies a bit more lemony.

3. In the bowl of a mixer, beat butter and lemon sugar on medium-high speed for 4 to 5 minutes, or until it is light and fluffy and the room smells like lemons. Beat in the egg, pausing to scrape down the bowl to make sure it's incorporated.

4. Reduce the mixer speed to slow and add flour, baking soda, salt, calendula petals, and crystallized ginger. Mix ever so briefly—under a minute will do.

5. Scoop tablespoons of dough 1 inch apart on the baking sheets. Bake for about 15 minutes, or just until the cookies turn golden brown. Cool on a wire rack. These cookies store well and last about 10 days in a tin.

¾ cup sugar
1 tablespoon lemon zest
½ cup (1 stick) unsalted butter, room temperature
1 egg
1¼ cups all-purpose flour
½ teaspoon baking soda
¼ teaspoon salt
⅓ cup calendula petals (from about 18 flowers)
¼ cup crystallized ginger,* finely diced

*Crystallized or candied ginger can be found in the baking aisle of most supermarkets; it's often shelved with dried fruits and nuts.

Dandelions

Botanical Name: *Taraxacum officinale*

Nicknames: swine snout, puffball, Irish daisy, and wet-the-bed flower (*pissenlit*)

Language of Flowers: Some say dandelions represent coquetry; others say they represent faithfulness and happiness. The meaning I like best is "wishes come true."

Background: This humble weed takes its name from the French *dent de lion*, or "tooth of the lion." Legend has it that the dandelion represents the sun, the moon, and the stars with its yellow flower, airy white puffball, and flying seeds. It opens its arms each morning and folds them again at day's end.

Culinary Use: The younger the better, fresh dandelion flowers have a sweet honeylike taste. The greens are commonly used in salads, and the root makes a cleansing and detoxifying diuretic tea. The butter-yellow flowers are most often used to make wine, but they have many uses in cooking and baking as well.

Seasonality: Dandelion flowers taste best and are most abundant in early spring but will hold bloom all through summer and into late autumn. Once plucked, they do not last. Clean and use them soon after harvesting.

Preparation: Ripe dandelions pull apart easily. For use in wine or tea, you can leave the flower head whole after clipping off the bitter green bottom. For jam, cookies, or cakes, you will want just the petals. Open each flower by tugging at the sides and then pull out the petals. Get ready for yellow fingers!

Measure: 1 cup dandelion petals = petals from about 40 to 60 blossoms.

Dandelion Wine

Dandelions are the bane of many a homeowner's existence, but they can be transformed into the most delicious sunshine-filled liqueur (colloquially called wine) by making a dandelion tea and then letting it ferment with sugar and citrus. You will find yourself creeping into neighbors' yards to pick more blossoms, it's just that good. *Makes about 1 gallon.*

1. Place dandelion flowers in a large heatproof container. Pour boiling water over top. Cover and let steep for at least 4 hours and up to 24 hours.

   When making dandelion wine, cleanliness is key. Make sure your kitchen counters, hands, and all utensils are sterile.

2. Pour the resulting tea through a fine-mesh strainer into a large pot or saucepan, pressing the petals to extract as much flavor as possible. Discard blossoms and bring tea to a boil.

3. Place sugar in a heatproof 1-gallon jar. Pour boiling dandelion tea into jar and stir to dissolve. Add lemon and orange slices. Cover jar and let liquid stand for 2 weeks at room temperature, shaking every couple days.

4. Pour dandelion wine through a fine-mesh strainer lined with a coffee filter into a clean container. Serve or cover and store refrigerated for up to 3 weeks.

4 cups dandelion flowers
6 cups boiling water
2½ cups sugar
1 Meyer lemon, thinly sliced
1 orange, thinly sliced

Fermenting Flower Wines

Some of the flowers that make lovely flower wines include pink (dianthus), lilac, lavender, daylily, elderflower, violet, tulip, herb flowers, roses, and pansies. Swap in equal amounts of whatever flowers you like, except for lavender; because it has a particularly strong flavor, lavender should always be used in slightly smaller amounts.

See page 181 for more recipes and tips.

Dandelion Muffins

Young dandelion blossoms have a sweet honeylike taste and fragrance that make for delicious muffins. I like them for breakfast or brunch, but you can easily bake this recipe in a loaf pan and use the bread for sandwiches. *Makes 24.*

1. Preheat oven to 375°F. Place paper liners in a muffin or cupcake tin or coat pan with nonstick spray.

2. In a large bowl, stir to combine flour, baking powder, salt, dandelion petals, apricots, and almonds. In a separate bowl, whisk milk, honey, and oil. Beat in the egg.

   Mixing muffin batter by hand prevents overmixing.

3. Add liquid ingredients to dry and mix by hand to combine. The batter should be wet. Pour into the prepared pan. Bake for 30 minutes, or until a toothpick inserted in the center of a muffin comes out clean. These muffins are best eaten the day they're made but can be kept for up to 3 days; if stored, they taste best toasted.

Dandelion Bread
Pour into a loaf pan and increase the baking time by 5 to 10 minutes, or until a toothpick inserted in the center comes out clean.

2 cups all-purpose flour
2 teaspoons baking powder
½ teaspoon salt
1 cup dandelion petals
⅓ cup dried apricots, finely chopped
⅓ cup almonds, chopped
1½ cups milk
4 tablespoons mild spring honey
¼ cup almond oil*
1 egg

*I love the taste of almond oil, but canola oil makes a fine substitute.

Dandelion butter is golden and delicious and so simple to make. (See page 178.)

Dandelion Blossom Cake

This confection is a simple variation on the hummingbird cake, a classic Southern layer cake that's studded with fruit and nuts. The addition of dandelion petals lends a sweet honey flavor that surely gives the hummingbirds something to search out. *Makes one 9-inch Bundt cake.*

1. Preheat oven to 350°F. Coat a Bundt pan with nonstick spray.

2. Smash bananas with a fork in a large mixing bowl. When no large chunks remain, stir in pineapple. Add sugar, honey, oil, and eggs and stir well to combine.

   If the bananas are not ripe enough to mash, use a food processor.

3. In another bowl, stir flour, baking powder, baking soda, cinnamon, salt, and dandelion petals until the petals are evenly dispersed. Fold into banana-pineapple mixture until just blended and no lumps remain. Gently fold in pecans and coconut if desired.

4. Pour cake batter into the prepared Bundt pan. Bake for 40 minutes, or until a metal tester inserted in the center comes out clean. Let cool on a wire rack for 15 minutes before turning the pan upside down and removing cake. Cool completely before spreading frosting on cake with an offset spatula.

This cake keeps incredibly well. Unfrosted, it can be stored in a cake dome or plastic zip-top bag at room temperature for up to 1 week. Frosted, it can be refrigerated in an airtight container for the same amount of time.

3 large ripe bananas, peeled and cut into chunks
1 cup pineapple chunks, canned and drained or fresh
¾ cup sugar
¾ cup honey
1 cup vegetable oil
3 eggs
2 cups all-purpose flour
2 teaspoons baking powder
1 teaspoon baking soda
½ teaspoon cinnamon
1 teaspoon salt
1 cup dandelion petals
½ cup pecans, chopped (optional)
½ cup sweetened flaked coconut (optional)
About 3 cups dandelion frosting (page 183)

Dandelion Fritters

Savory or sweet: it's your choice. This recipe swings both ways. Make these fritters savory with a little cayenne and freshly ground pepper. Or make them as a dessert, adding a pinch of cinnamon and sugar and some maple syrup for dipping. *Serves 6.*

1. In a large, heavy-bottomed pot over high heat, warm oil to 375°F.

2. Whisk to combine milk and egg in a small bowl. In a medium bowl, stir to combine flour, cornmeal, salt, and the optional ingredients for the flavor you have chosen (savory or sweet).

3. Gently dip each dandelion blossom in milk mixture and then dredge in flour mixture to coat.

4. Carefully place battered flowers into hot oil and fry for about 3 minutes, or until golden brown. Place fritters on a paper towel to blot the excess oil. Serve with or without maple syrup.

1 cup canola oil
1 cup milk
1 egg, beaten
¾ cup all-purpose flour
¼ cup cornmeal*
½ teaspoon salt
⅛ teaspoon freshly ground pepper
   (for savory fritters)
¼ teaspoon cayenne pepper
   (for savory fritters)
¼ teaspoon cinnamon (for sweet
   fritters)
1 tablespoon sugar (for sweet fritters)
3 to 4 cups dandelion blossoms
   (about 60 flowers)
Maple syrup for serving, if desired

*Finely ground cornmeal is ideal if you want these to be sweet. For savory fritters, coarsely ground cornmeal is preferred.

Dandelion Ham-and-Egg Cups

If you ask me, brunch is the ideal meal. Unfussy and packed full of protein (but just as friendly toward sweets), it is a repast full of smiles. I make ham-and-egg cups for brunch all the time, and this variation with dandelion blossoms tucked in makes for a great rendition of a classic. *Makes 12.*

1. Preheat oven to 350°F. Line each cup in a muffin pan with 2 pieces of ham, overlapping so there are no holes.

2. Break an egg into the center of each cup. Top each with a generous pinch of dandelion petals and a crumble of goat cheese, if desired. Gently slide pan into oven and bake for about 15 minutes, or until eggs no longer jiggle when pan is moved.

3. Let cool on a wire rack for 5 minutes before transferring cups to a serving plate. Just before serving, sprinkle salt and pepper over top.

24 slices ham*
8 eggs
½ cup dandelion petals
About 1 cup (¼ pound) soft goat
   cheese, crumbled (optional)
¼ teaspoon sea salt
¼ teaspoon freshly ground pepper

*Any deli ham will work; try a nice maple-glazed ham in a medium cut. Nitrate-free organic ham is another favorite of mine.

Dandelion Cookies

Crunchy, chewy, and honey flavored, these mammoth cookies make my mouth water. They are the perfect accompaniment to a glass of milk as an afternoon snack. Just one bite will assure them a permanent spot in your picnic basket. *Makes 12 extra-large cookies.*

1. Preheat oven to 350°F. Line 2 baking sheets with parchment paper.

2. In a medium bowl, stir to combine flour, oats, baking soda, and allspice.

3. Beat butter, sugar, molasses and vanilla with a mixer on medium speed for 4 to 5 minutes, or until smooth and light in color. Add egg and beat until fully incorporated. Stop the mixer and scrape the sides of the bowl once during mixing.

4. Blend dry ingredients, dandelion petals, and apricots into butter mixture and mix just enough so that any streaks of flour disappear.

5. Scoop 2-inch balls of batter 2 inches apart onto prepared baking sheets. Bake until the house smells like honeyed oatmeal and the cookies have spread but are still flexible, about 12 minutes. These cookies keep for one week in an airtight container, but I dare you to make them last that long.

Make-Ahead Dandelion Cookies
You can portion the batter with an ice-cream scoop onto a parchment-paper-lined baking sheet and freeze the dough balls. Once they are frozen, store them for up to 2 months and bake one or more at a time.

1¼ cups all-purpose flour
1⅓ cups oats
1 teaspoon baking soda
¼ teaspoon allspice
½ cup (1 stick) unsalted butter, room temperature
1 cup sugar
2 tablespoons molasses
1 teaspoon pure vanilla extract
1 egg
1 cup dandelion petals
3 ounces dried apricots, chopped in small dice

Daylilies

Botanical Name: *Hemerocallis fulva*

Nicknames: Outhouse lily

Language of Flowers: Daylilies symbolize coquetry and rebirth; in the Chinese language of flowers, they symbolize the mother.

Background: These fleeting flowers got their name from the Greek *hemera*, for "day," and *kalles*, for "beauty." Each flower lasts for only one day, but another replaces it the next. Daylilies derive their nickname of "outhouse lily" from the location they were commonly planted. In New England, when attempting to discover remains of old homesteads, historians often look for clumps of daylilies in wooded areas because they were so often planted along the foundations of outhouses.

Culinary Use: All parts of the flower are edible, including the early spring leaves, the flower buds and blooms, and even the roots. The buds taste of the color green—fresh and poppy—while the flowers taste like sweet lettuce, with no bitter aftertaste. Daylily buds are used in stir-fries and sautées, and the flowers are most often used in salads. Daylilies are common in Chinese cooking and are sold dried as "golden needles." You can add the petals to egg dishes, soups, and salads or dip whole flowers in batter and fry them, as you would squash blossoms (page 147).

Seasonality: Daylily buds and blooms can be harvested throughout summer, depending on the variety and its bloom time. Daylilies are tough plants that naturalize easily. They prefer sun but are mindless of their soil. They are often found in open meadows or along roadsides and railroad tracks.

Preparation: Daylily buds will keep in the refrigerator for several days, but the delicate flowers (trumpet-shaped blooms that grow in multiples on a leafless stalk) should be consumed the day they are picked. The buds and petals can be plucked, carefully washed, and laid on a paper towel to dry.

Measure: 1 cup daylily petals = petals from about 6 flowers.

Gouda Cheddar Daylily Biscuits

I cannot resist a good cheese. Add a little butter and I'm yours. Because of their bright, sweet flavor of daylilies, it was inevitable they would find their way into these irresistible cheese biscuits. *Makes 12 biscuits.*

1. Preheat oven to 425°F. Combine flour, baking powder, baking soda, and salt in the bowl of a food processor and pulse several times. Add butter and pulse until the mixture has mostly pea-size lumps. Turn it into a medium bowl and, using your hands, gently mix in buttermilk, egg, daylily petals, Gouda, cheddar, and chives.

2. Put about 3 tablespoons of butter into a 10-inch cast iron skillet and place it in the oven until the butter melts. Swirl the melted butter in the pan to coat the bottom; pour most of the butter out of the pan and into a cup. Drop 12 dollops of dough in the skillet and brush the tops with the reserved melted butter.

3. Bake for 18 to 20 minutes, until the tops are irresistibly golden brown and a tester inserted in the center of a biscuit comes out clean. Cool biscuits on a wire rack for 5 minutes. Serve hot.

A Daylily Brunch

You could make a whole morning meal with daylilies: try these biscuits, daylily scrambled eggs (made according to the recipe on page 14, but with daylilies), and fruit salad served in daylily cups as the base for a fabulous theme meal. Add the poor man's asparagus (page 40) and you've even got your "vegetable"!

2 cups all-purpose flour
2 teaspoons baking powder
½ teaspoon baking soda
½ teaspoon salt
8 tablespoons (1 stick) very cold unsalted butter, cubed, plus more for the pan and biscuit tops
1 cup buttermilk
1 egg
1 cup daylily petals (from about 6 flowers), chopped
¾ cup smoked Gouda, shredded
¼ cup aged cheddar, shredded
¼ cup finely diced chives

Daylily Petal Salad

Daylilies are a fleeting treasure, here today and gone tomorrow—literally. A quick salad captures their color and fresh, sweet flavor. Invite some friends and linger over a daylily salad for lunch. If you like, add a little shredded crabmeat or some tuna to make it a full meal. *Serves 4.*

Put arugula in a shallow serving bowl. Arrange sliced avocado, daylily petals, and Gouda over top. Sprinkle salad with olive oil and lemon juice and toss gently. Top with salt and pepper and serve immediately.

4 cups arugula
1 avocado, pitted and slivered
Petals of 6 daylily flowers
⅓ cup (about 1 ounce) aged Gouda, shaved
3 tablespoons extra-virgin olive oil
2 teaspoons freshly squeezed lemon juice
¼ teaspoon flaky sea salt
Freshly ground black pepper, to taste

Daylily Cheesecake

Pie and cheesecake are two of my older son's favorite food groups, so I knew this one had to have his seal of approval. He generally likes a plain New York–style cheesecake with a traditional graham cracker crust—no nonsense. But he also loves this simple daylily version: the flecks of petal resemble zest and add a slight green note to both the crust and the light, creamy cheesecake. *Makes one 9-inch cake.*

1. Preheat oven to 350°F. Line a 9-inch springform pan with parchment paper.

2. Pulse to combine all crust ingredients in a food processor, then whir until mixture is homogenous. Press mixture into the bottom of the prepared pan and bake for 20 to 25 minutes, or until it's golden brown and smells of nutty, buttery goodness. Let cool.

3. Raise oven temperature to 450°F. In the bowl of a mixer, beat cream cheese, sugar, vanilla, and lemon on medium-high speed for 6 to 8 minutes, or until smooth. With mixer on low speed, add eggs one at a time, scraping the sides of the bowl to make sure mixture is well blended. Mix on medium speed for 1 minute more until batter is thick and creamy. Add daylilies and beat to combine.

4. Spoon cheesecake into the cooled crust. Bake for 10 minutes, or until the cake is puffed and just starting to brown. Reduce oven temperature to 250°F and bake for about 1 hour, or until the outside is firm but the middle is still slightly loose when shaken. Mix sour cream with sugar, pour topping over cake, and bake for 10 minutes more.

5. Let cheesecake cool to room temperature. Run a knife around the edge to loosen it. Cover cake loosely with plastic wrap. Refrigerate overnight before serving.

Plan Ahead
Bake cheesecake at least 1 day before serving so it has time to chill in the refrigerator and the flavors can meld. Chilled, it keeps well for about 1 week.

CRUST
¼ cup (½ stick) unsalted butter, melted
¼ cup packed light or dark brown sugar*
2 tablespoons sugar
3 tablespoons chopped daylilies
1 cup all-purpose flour
⅔ cup pecans

CHEESECAKE
2½ pounds cream cheese,** room temperature
1½ cups sugar
2 teaspoons pure vanilla extract
1 teaspoon lemon zest
6 eggs
½ cup daylilies, finely chopped

TOPPING
2 cups sour cream
3 tablespoons sugar

*Though light brown sugar is more common, I prefer dark brown sugar for its rich, moist qualities. You can use either.

**Use a good-quality cream cheese like Philadelphia brand; I promise you'll be happier.

Roasted Daylily Buds

Known as "poor man's asparagus," roasted daylilies taste like a milder version of that vegetable. I only say this recipe serves two because harvesting enough daylily buds for more than two people can be tricky. But you can take note of all your friends who have daylilies in their yards and invite them over for a BYOB ("bring your own buds") party. *Serves 2.*

Preheat oven to 400°F. Toss daylily buds on a baking sheet and jiggle the olive oil and sea salt over the top. Roast for 5 minutes, until glistening and slightly tender. Eat immediately.

For extra flavor, try drizzling roasted daylily buds with 2 tablespoons calendula butter or herb flower butter (page 178). Or add 4 cloves garlic before roasting and/or 2 tablespoons Parmesan cheese immediately after.

2 cups daylily buds (about 20 buds),*
    still tightly closed
2 tablespoons extra-virgin olive oil
Pinch sea salt

*Daylily blossoms must be used the day they are harvested, but the buds last for about a week in the refrigerator. So you may gather them over that time and cook them all at once.

Small young daylily buds are tastier—just like young asparagus—so look for ones that are about 2 inches long.

Daylily Curry

Daylilies are commonly used in Asian cooking, so it's no stretch of the imagination to spice them up with an Indian curry. I like a little shrimp with this dish, but you can easily keep it vegetarian or substitute poultry or meat. *Serves 4.*

1. Warm oil in a large skillet over low heat. Stir curry powder into oil until the fragrance is released.

2. Add garlic, onion, carrots, and celery and cook, stirring occasionally, for about 5 minutes, or until the onion wilts.

3. Stir in shrimp, coconut milk, basil, lime juice, salt, and chicken stock. Cook for 1 minute more, then add daylily petals and cashews. Continue to cook, stirring occasionally, until shrimp is pink and cooked through. Serve over hot rice.

Dried daylilies are available all year long. If you have a hankering for this curry in the "off season," have no fear. If there's an Asian market near you, you can buy dried daylilies, which are a key ingredient in classic recipes like hot and sour soup. Known as "golden needles," dried daylilies merely need to be plumped in warm water for 20 minutes before using. Save them for the savory dishes—they are fantastic for this curry, but you could throw them into almost any stir-fry; in the autumn, they work really well in squash or carrot soups.

2 tablespoons vegetable oil

3 tablespoons curry powder

3 cloves garlic, minced

1 onion, sliced in quarter moons

2 carrots, sliced ¼ inch thick diagonally

4 celery stalks, sliced ¼ inch thick diagonally

½ pound shrimp, cleaned

1 (14-ounce) can coconut milk

Leaves from 1 stem basil (about 12 leaves, or scant ¼ cup)

Juice of 1 lime

¼ teaspoon salt

¼ cup chicken stock

2 cups daylily petals (from about 12 flowers)*

½ cup cashews

2 cups jasmine rice, cooked according to package instructions**

*You may substitute daylily buds for the blossoms, but they don't need to cook as long, so add them when you add the shrimp.

**Feel free to substitute the rice of your choice, be it long-grain basmati, short-grain brown, or whatever you like.

Dianthus

Botanical Name: *Dianthus*

Nicknames: Pink (or pinks), sweet William, carnation, and gillyflower (Shakespeare)

Language of Flowers: Dianthus stands for love, fascination, distinction, and pure affection.

Background: The first time I saw dianthus, I fell in love. I had no idea they were related to carnations. Their gray foliage and variously colored flowers have centers that look like an eye just opened to look into yours. The word *dianthus* likely comes from the Greek *dios* (god) and *anthos* (flower). The common name

carnation is possibly a misspelling of the word *coronation*, for dianthus was among the blossoms used to weave coronation crowns.

Although one would think the nickname "pink" derives from the color of the bloom, the opposite is true. The color pink gets its name from the color of the flower, and pinking shears are so named because they create a fringe like the ruffled-petal edging on this long-beloved flower.

Culinary Use: Dianthus is sweet with a slightly clovelike aftertaste. The petals are used in salads and are an ingredient in the liqueur Chartreuse.

Seasonality: In bloom from late spring through midsummer, dianthus can be grown in containers or a backyard either from seed or starter plants.

Preparation: You need to gather a lot of dianthus flowers to have a good amount of petals, so patience is a virtue. Wash and dry the flowers. Release the petals by holding the flower by its calyx (the green base) and tugging the petals loose. The white part of the petal is a bit bitter, so you may want to snip it off with kitchen scissors.

Measure: 1 cup dianthus petals = petals from about 50 to 70 flowers.

Pickled Pink Petals

Though this recipe is made with more than just the petals of pinks, I couldn't resist the urge to alliterate. Pepquino pickles are refreshing and cooling and make a great addition to a cheese plate or a burger, especially when they're pickled with pinks. *Makes 1 quart.*

1. In a clean 1-quart jar, layer dianthus petals with pepquinos, corn, and brown sugar all the way to the top.

2. In a medium saucepan over medium heat, simmer vinegar, cloves, coriander, bay leaves, and cinnamon for 10 minutes. Pour the hot vinegar mixture into the jar. Cap tightly and refrigerate for 2 weeks before eating. Store for up to 2 months in the refrigerator.

Pick a Peck of Pickled Pinks

Adapt this recipe to use vegetables you love or have in overabundance. Try swapping out the pepquinos for any of the following: 2 pickling cucumbers, skinned and thinly sliced; 1½ cups cauliflower; 1½ cups baby onions; or 2 cups green beans.

4 cups dianthus petals
3 cups pepquinos*
Kernels from 2 ears of corn (about 1½ cups)
2 cups packed light brown sugar
2 cups white wine vinegar
6 cloves
2 teaspoons coriander seeds
2 bay leaves
1 cinnamon stick

*Pepquinos may look like mini watermelons but they're really a type of cucumber that's tasty fresh or pickled. Once hard to find, pepquinos are becoming widely available at farm stands and from specialty growers.

Sweet William Shortbread

I like a sweet that is not too sweet and has just the right amount of complexity to make it interesting. Dianthus is a good choice for shortbread because, even though it has a somewhat perfumy flavor, the clove undertone sneaks in to balance the sweet floral notes. Call it a biscuit and pair it with a hard cheese. *Makes 24 cookies.*

1. Lay a 14-by-18-inch sheet of parchment paper on your counter.

2. Toss flours and salt into the bowl of a food processor and pulse about 5 times to combine. Add butter, sugar, and vanilla and process for 1 to 2 minutes, until the mixture forms a ball.

3. Lightly flour a clean workspace and turn the dough onto it. Gently mix in dianthus petals with your hands. At this point the dough will be a little tacky, but don't worry. Transfer it to the parchment paper and make a log about 18 inches long and 2 inches thick. Roll parchment to encase the log and refrigerate it for 2 hours or freeze it for at least 2 hours and up to 1 month.

4. Preheat oven to 325°F. Line a baking sheet with parchment paper.

   You can reuse the parchment paper the dough was wrapped in to line your baking sheet.

5. Cut shortbread into 1/4-inch-thick slices and place them on the prepared baking sheet 1 inch apart. Bake for 20 minutes, or until shortbread is golden brown around the edges; halfway through baking, you can decorate with more flowers as indicated below. Place on a wire rack to cool. Store remainders in an airtight container for up to 10 days.

Top with flowers
Halfway through baking, you can remove the pan from the oven, place a whole dianthus flower (or a few petals) on each cookie, brush a little egg white over top to help them stick, and return them to the oven to finish baking.

Try herb flowers or apricots
A mix of herb flowers or roughly chopped dried apricots works well in this sweet-yet-savory cookie.

2 cups all-purpose flour
1/4 cup almond flour*
1/8 teaspoon salt
1 cup (2 sticks) unsalted butter, room temperature
1/2 cup sugar
1/2 teaspoon pure vanilla extract
2 tablespoons dianthus petals, plus more for decorating (optional)
1 egg white, for decorating (optional)

*Almond flour, sometimes sold as almond meal, is used as a substitute for flour in many gluten-free recipes (though that is not the case here). Almond meal is high in protein, has a low glycemic index (it's low in sugar), and is low in carbs. All that and it adds a crumbly, nutty, natural sweetness to the dough. If you can't find it, try coconut flour.

Dianthus Spiced Chocolate Cookies

Sometimes chocolate just begs for a little spice. I prefer chile in my chocolate, and a little salt never hurts, either. For this reason, I like baking dianthus in a crisp chocolate cookie: it looks so delicate, with its fringes and ruffles all pink and pretty, but then the flavor hits and it has a bit of spice and warmth—very "sugar and spice and everything nice." *Makes about 36 cookies.*

1. Lay a 14-by-18-inch sheet of parchment paper on your counter.

2. Combine flour, cocoa, salt, pepper, cinnamon, cayenne, and cloves in a medium bowl and fluff mixture with a fork until evenly distributed.

3. Beat butter in the bowl of a mixer just to soften it. Add sugar and beat on medium-high speed for 3 minutes, or until mixture is light and soft. Add dianthus petals, egg, and vanilla and beat for about 3 more minutes, or until smooth; be sure to scrape the sides of the bowl once or twice while mixing. With mixer on low speed, gradually add flour mixture. Mix just until the dough is combined and no flour streaks remain.

4. Turn out dough onto the parchment. Spread it into a log about 1 inch in diameter and 12 inches long. Wrap parchment around it to seal. Refrigerate for at least 2 hours or freeze in an airtight bag for up to 2 months.

5. Preheat oven to 350°F. Line a baking sheet with parchment paper.

6. Brush dough log with egg white and sprinkle sanding sugar over the entire surface. Slice dough into 1/4-inch rounds and place them about 1 inch apart on the prepared baking sheet. Bake about 12 minutes, or until dough dulls in color and smells good. Let cookies cool on the sheet for about 5 minutes before moving them to a wire rack to cool completely. These beauties will keep for about 5 days in a tin.

1½ cups all-purpose flour
¾ cup cocoa powder
¼ teaspoon salt
¼ teaspoon pepper
¼ teaspoon cinnamon
¼ teaspoon cayenne pepper
Pinch ground cloves
¾ cup (1½ sticks) unsalted butter, room temperature
1 cup sugar
⅓ cup dianthus petals
1 egg
1½ teaspoons pure vanilla extract
Sanding sugar, for decorating

The dough for this recipe freezes so well, you might want to make a double batch. Bake one log and freeze the other for later.

Pink Tuiles

These delicate, crispy cookies are named after the French roof tiles (*tuiles*) they resemble. Speckled with pink petals, this version of the classic is too pretty to resist. *Makes about 18 cookies.*

1. Pulverize dianthus petals with confectioners' sugar in a food processor.

2. With a mixer on medium-high speed, cream butter with the sugar just until they come together. Gradually beat in egg whites. With mixer on low speed, gradually add flour and salt and blend for 2 minutes until no lumps remain. Be careful not to overmix the batter. Cover the mixing bowl and leave it in the refrigerator for 1 hour or more.

3. Preheat oven to 350°F. Line 3 baking sheets with parchment paper or silicone mats and butter them well. (This is one case where nonstick spray is not a good stand-in for butter.)

4. Dollop about 2 tablespoons batter per cookie and space them several inches apart on the prepared baking sheets. (I make about 3 per baking sheet.) Use an offset spatula to spread the batter into nice even 3-inch circles.

5. Bake cookies one sheet at a time for 5 to 8 minutes, or until the edges are golden and the centers just begin to brown. As soon as they come out of the oven, shape tuiles by draping them over a cup, rolling pin, or wine bottle for 20 to 30 seconds (until set), or try hand rolling them into "cigars" or cones (place these seam side down to cool). Get creative, work fast, and try to pretend your fingers aren't burning! Eat within a few hours or store in airtight containers for several days.

¼ cup dianthus petals,* plus more for decorating if desired
½ cup confectioners' sugar
¼ cup (2 tablespoons) unsalted butter, plus more for baking
2 egg whites, room temperature
½ cup sifted cake flour
Pinch salt

*Pinks are perfect, but you can also make these cookies with other flowers such as pansies, rose petals, geraniums, dandelions, or lavender flowers. If using lavender, reduce the amount to 2 teaspoons. (It's potent stuff.)

Molded on cups, flower tuiles make fantastic bowls for ice creams. They are especially good with chamomile crème fraîche ice cream, lavender honey ice cream, or rose petal ice cream (pages 77 and 185). They are also a nice simple dessert, served alongside a flavored whipped cream, such as rose, geranium, or herb flower, topped with fresh berries.

Pink Rosé Wine Cake

Dianthus is one of the 130 secret herbs and flowers used by monks at the Chartreuse monastery to make their signature liqueur. So, in the spirit of that long-standing tradition, let's pair the flower's pink petals with rosé wine for a delightfully tipsy cake. *Makes one 9-inch cake.*

1. Preheat oven to 350°F. Line a 9-inch cake pan with parchment paper and coat it with nonstick spray.

2. Beat butter and sugar in the bowl of a mixer until mixture is soft, light, and fluffy, about 4 minutes. While waiting for butter and sugar to fluff, sift flour with baking powder, baking soda, and salt.

3. Add eggs, one at a time, making sure the first is fully incorporated before adding the next. Scrape down the paddle and the sides of the bowl as needed to make sure everything is fully incorporated. You can multitask again by fluffing dianthus petals into flour. Toss vanilla into butter mixture and beat on medium-high speed for about 30 seconds.

4. Beat flour mixture and wine into butter mixture in 3 alternating additions, starting and ending with flour mixture. When it's all in, turn mixer off and gently stir in cherries.

5. Pour batter into the prepared pan and bake until a tester inserted in the center comes out clean, about 45 minutes. Serve with dianthus-infused whipped cream and/or candied dianthus flowers, if desired, or store cake for up to 3 days.

I cook with local ingredients whenever possible, and on the North Fork of Long Island, that means using locally produced wine or beer. It's become something we are known for at Mali B—whether it's flavoring cake pops, brownies, wedding cakes, cookies, or brittles, wine makes a regular appearance in our roster. It adds depth of flavor to baked goods, and most (but not all) of the alcohol is baked off in the oven.

½ cup (1 stick) unsalted butter, room temperature
¾ cup sugar
1½ cups sifted all-purpose flour
1½ teaspoons baking powder
½ teaspoon baking soda
¼ teaspoon salt
2 eggs
4 tablespoons dianthus petals, coarsely chopped
2 teaspoons pure vanilla extract
⅔ cup rosé wine
1½ cups cherries, pitted
Dianthus whipped cream (page 183) for topping (optional)
Candied dianthus flowers (page 176), for topping (optional)

The spicy sweetness of the flower complements a crisp rosé, and cherries add a third layer of pink. Three pinks!

Elderflowers

Botanical Name: *Sambucus nigra*

Nicknames: Pipe tree

Language of Flowers: Elderflowers represent compassion.

Background: The elder (also known as elderberry) tree has long been considered magical. When I was first taught about this plant, I was told that to pick it, one had to leave a piece of oneself (such as a strand of hair) in tribute. I didn't realize until later that this was because of beliefs that the elder is associated with witches and that an elder tree might be a witch in disguise.

The cross that Jesus was crucified on was made of elder, which is why some say this tree does not stand up straight and tall like other trees. Elder makes appearances in the writings of Pliny and Hippocrates and is referenced in literature as far back as the 1300s. The components of elder are renowned in Native American medicines for healing colds and flus.

Culinary Use: Elderflower tastes of licorice. It is sweet and, if used too heavy-handedly, can be overwhelming. Subtlety is key. Historically, elderflower's most common use was as a cordial, and tales of its use date back thousands of years. Today it is still commonly used in cordials and liqueurs like St. Germain. Elder is widely used to boost the immune system. The berry is perhaps the part of the plant most widely used for its immunity-enhancing properties, but a tisane—such as elderflower tea, page 181—made from its flower works well, too.

Seasonality: In much of North America, elderflowers bloom for a short period beginning in early spring: from mid-May through the beginning of June.

Preparation: Elderflowers are particularly good at collecting insects. The best way to get rid of them is to immerse the flowers in salt water, swish them around, and rinse them again with fresh water. Elderflowers cannot be eaten raw; they must be cooked. Cook fresh or dried elderflowers in teas, simple syrups, and other staples that can then be used in baked goods, cocktails, or whatever you please.

Measure: 1 cup elderflowers = about 13 flowers (used whole), or ⅓ cup dried elderflowers.

Elderflower Fruit Salad

In this recipe, we'll use the simple syrup as a complement to fresh fruit. Fresh berries and melons are the perfect base for a little elderflower pick-me-up and provide a fresh spin on a naked fruit salad. *Serves 4 to 6.*

Toss fruits together in a large bowl. Toss in mint and drizzle syrup over the top. Gently mix in syrup, and spoon fruit salad into individual serving bowls.

1 small cantaloupe, balled (3 cups)
¼ watermelon, balled (2 cups)
½ pint fresh raspberries (1 cup)
½ pint fresh blackberries (1 cup)
½ pint fresh blueberries (1 cup)
1 sprig of mint, leaves removed and
   sliced chiffonade style*
¼ cup elderflower simple syrup
   (page 177)

*Pull the leaves off the mint, stack them, and roll them. Then slice the roll thinly, yielding nice clean strips.

Elderflower simple syrup is sweetly fragrant, with a light licorice scent. It pairs perfectly with summer melons and berries, and it's also delicious mixed with a little sparkling wine for a refreshing beverage.

Almond Elderflower Pound Cake

Almonds and elderflowers pair beautifully and add a note of complexity to this simple, delicious pound cake. It's the perfect cake to pull out of your hat if you need something to bring to a friend's house or to send a gift or to toast for breakfast . . . Oh, let me count the ways it will come in handy. *Makes one 9-by-5-by-3-inch loaf.*

1 (7-ounce) package almond paste
1 cup sugar
2 cups all-purpose flour, divided
1 cup (2 sticks) room-temperature unsalted butter, cubed
2 tablespoons elderflower simple syrup (page 177)
4 eggs
1 teaspoon baking powder
½ cup milk

1. Preheat oven to 325°F. Butter a 9-by-5-by-3-inch loaf pan and sift a little bit of flour on the bottom and sides.

2. Put almond paste in the bowl of a food processor. Add sugar and ½ cup of the flour and pulse until the mixture resembles coarse sand. Add butter and elderflower syrup and pulse until the mixture resembles marbles or peas. Add eggs one at a time, processing after each addition.

3. Combine the remaining 1½ cups flour with baking powder in a bowl. Gradually mix in half the flour mixture, then the milk, and then the remainder of the flour mixture.

4. Pour batter into the prepared loaf pan and bake for about 1 hour. The house will smell like sweet almonds, and when it's done a tester inserted into the cake will come out clean. Cool cake on a wire rack for about 10 minutes in the pan; then turn it out onto the rack to cool completely.

If you wish to save this cake, it stores for up to 1 week in an airtight container in the fridge. If wrapped in plastic wrap and then in foil, it can be frozen for 1 month.

Elderflower Marshmallows

At Mali B, we make lots of marshmallows and we make them in lots of varieties. We have our signature flavors, such as green tea and beer, and our standards, like vanilla bean and salted dulce de leche. And then we have our seasonals, which range wildly and are often available only for a few weeks each year. Elderflower is one of those special flavors. That said, we occasionally cheat and use dried elderflowers to make these mallows off-season. *Makes one 9-inch sheet of marshmallow to be cut however you like.*

1. Coat a 9-inch square pan with nonstick spray.

2. Pour 1/2 cup of the elderflower tea into the bowl of a mixer fitted with the whisk attachment. Sprinkle gelatin over the tea.

3. Heat the remaining 1/2 cup tea, corn syrup, sugar, and salt in a heavy-bottom pot over high heat. Boil mixture until the temperature reaches 240°F. With the mixer on low speed, slowly and carefully beat in hot syrup mixture. When it's fully incorporated, turn the mixer to high speed and watch the mixture grow in volume; it will go from liquid to thick white ribbons in 10 to 15 minutes. Continue to beat until it turns opaque and begins to pull away from the sides of the bowl.

4. Use a flexible spatula to quickly scrape marshmallow into the prepared pan. Sift confectioners' sugar in an even layer over the top. Let the mallow set (or cure) in the pan overnight.

5. Put about 1/2 cup confectioners' sugar in a bowl and dust a cutting board with more confectioners' sugar. Flip marshmallow slab onto the cutting board. You can use a knife, a pizza cutter, or a cookie cutter. As you cut the shapes, toss them in confectioners' sugar to coat the sticky sides. Store in an airtight container for up to 2 weeks.

1 cup elderflower tea (page 181), divided
3 (3/4-ounce) packets gelatin
1 cup light corn syrup
1½ cups sugar
¼ teaspoon salt
Confectioners' sugar, for dusting

Flower Marshmallows

It's easy to flavor lovely homemade marshmallows with most any edible flower. Just make flower tea according to the recipe on page 181 and use it instead of elderflower tea in this mallow recipe. I like violet, chamomile, rose, and nasturtium.

Elderflower Lemon Cakelets

Lemon, tart and refreshing, works well with delicate and sweet elder. Graced with elderflower tea in both the cake and the glaze, these tasty cakelets are the perfect guilt-free picnic or lunchbox treat. *Makes 12 cakelets.*

1. Preheat oven to 325°F. Coat the inside of a 12-cup mini Bundt cake pan with nonstick spray.

2. Beat butter and sugar with a mixer on high speed for 5 minutes, or until mixture is palest yellow and fluffy looking. Add eggs one at a time, scraping down the bowl of the mixer after each addition and making sure one egg is fully incorporated before adding the next, mixing about 6 minutes in all.

3. Sift together flour, baking powder, baking soda, and salt in a bowl.

4. With the mixer on low speed, beat in dry ingredients and yogurt in 3 alternating additions, beginning and ending with dry ingredients. Fold in lemon zest and elderflower tea and mix just until the batter comes together and no flour streaks remain.

5. Spoon cake batter into the prepared pan and bake for about 20 minutes, or until a tester inserted in the center comes out clean. Turn cakes onto a wire cooling rack set over parchment paper or a baking sheet (something easy to clean!).

6. To make the glaze, simply whisk together confectioners' sugar, lemon juice, and elderflower tea until no lumps remain. Pour over the cakelets, allowing the glaze to be absorbed. Eat right away if you can't resist, or wait until the cakelets cool. Store them in an airtight container for up to 4 days.

One Big Elderflower Lemon Cake

You can make this recipe in a regular Bundt cake pan, just increase the baking time to about 35 minutes.

CAKE

1 cup (2 sticks) unsalted butter, room temperature
3 cups sugar
6 eggs
2¾ cups cake flour
¼ teaspoon baking powder
¼ teaspoon baking soda
¼ teaspoon salt
1 cup Greek yogurt
1 teaspoon freshly grated lemon zest
2 tablespoons elderflower tea (page 181)

GLAZE

2 cups confectioners' sugar
1 teaspoon lemon juice
3 to 4 tablespoons elderflower tea (page 181)

Elderflower Blueberry Cobbler

Cobblers are so friendly and unfussy—they practically beckon you with cartoon-style fingers of aroma from the oven. In this recipe, the earthy tartness of the blueberries is complemented by the floral sweetness of the elderflower. Add a biscuit topping and some whipped cream, and you have a bit of summer heaven. *Makes one 9-by-13-inch pan, serves 6 to 8.*

1. Preheat oven to 375°F. Coat a 9-by-13-inch baking dish with nonstick spray.

2. Into the baking dish, toss blueberries, flour, sugar, elderflower tea, lemon juice, and cardamom.

3. In a bowl mix together flour, cornmeal, baking powder, and 1/3 cup of the sugar. Cut butter into flour mixture with a fork, making certain that it's well broken up and coated. Keep the topping rather chunky; large pea-size pieces are what you are looking for. Add milk and stir with a fork just until mixture becomes a thick batter that is uniformly moist. Drop dollops of batter over blueberries until they are covered.

4. Mix remaining 2 teaspoons sugar with cinnamon and sprinkle it over top. Bake cobbler for 25 minutes, or until berries are bubbling and a toothpick inserted into the center of one of the dollops of dough comes out clean. Cool briefly before topping with whipped cream and serving.

If necessary, you can store baked cobbler in the refrigerator for up to 2 days. It tastes best warm, so be sure to reheat briefly before eating.

FRUIT BOTTOM

4 cups (2 pints) blueberries*
1 tablespoon all-purpose flour
1/2 cup sugar
2 tablespoons elderflower tea
 (page 181)
2 tablespoons lemon juice
1/4 teaspoon cardamom

BISCUIT TOPPING

1 1/2 cups all-purpose flour
1/4 cup finely ground cornmeal
1 tablespoon plus 1 teaspoon baking
 powder
1/3 cup plus 2 teaspoons sugar, divided
4 tablespoons (1/2 stick) unsalted
 butter, still cool to the touch and
 cut into small cubes
3/4 cup cold milk
1/2 teaspoon cinnamon
3 cups elderflower whipped cream
 (page 183)

*This recipe works equally well with blackberries, apricots, and peaches.

Geraniums

Botanical Name: *Pelargonium*

Nicknames: Cranesbill

Language of Flowers: The scented geranium was important in Victorian bouquets, and different scents have different meanings: rose means preference, lemon indicates unexpected meeting, nutmeg stands for expected meeting, and oak leaf signifies true friendship or "deign to smile." A gift of an oak leaf seals a friendship.

Background: The English name cranesbill comes from the shape of the fruit—exposed when the petals drop—which resembles a crane's bill. In Celtic legend, the crane symbolized wisdom.

Culinary Use: For culinary use, be sure to select scented geraniums; avoid common geraniums (botanical name *Geranium*), which are edible but contain little flavor. The flower of the scented geranium is somewhat unremarkable. It is the leaf that gives off the bulk of the flavor and scent. Individual species have their own unique scent, ranging from rose to lemon to chocolate mint to citronella to orange and everything in between. They make lovely jellies, flavored sugars, and teas.

Seasonality: Geraniums bloom from late spring through early autumn.

Preparation: Geraniums give off few flowers, and sporadically at that. But the good news is that, because the leaves are far more powerfully scented than the flowers, you can always substitute the leaves for the flowers. To harvest, pluck the blossoms when they first open and use only the petals, discarding the center and stalk. Cut the leaves as you would any edible greens, and (as always) be certain they are washed and dried before you use them.

Measure: 1 cup geranium petals = petals from about 40 to 60 flowers.

Chocolate-Dipped Orange Geranium Cookies

These subtle but satisfying cookies are inspired by my in-laws: Jason loves orange and chocolate, and my dear mother-in-law, Iris, loves nothing more than a good cookie. She regularly stops by the kitchen in hopes that we have deemed a cookie just a little too brown to go out, since that is her favorite. *Makes 36 cookies.*

1. Have a large sheet of parchment paper ready on your work surface.

2. With a mixer on medium speed, beat butter and sugar for 3 minutes, or until smooth and creamy. Add egg and beat until smooth. Beat in vanilla.

3. Sift flour, baking soda, and cream of tartar into a medium bowl. Stir in geranium petals. Gradually beat flour mixture into butter mixture. Turn dough onto parchment paper. Roll it into a 2-inch round log, wrap in the parchment, and refrigerate it for at least 2 hours and up to overnight.

4. Preheat oven to 350°F and line 2 baking sheets with parchment paper. Unwrap dough and cut it into ¼-inch-thick slices. Place slices 2 inches apart on prepared baking sheets. Bake cookies for about 10 minutes, or until the edges are golden brown. Let cookies cool slightly on baking sheets before transferring them to a wire rack to cool completely.

5. In a double boiler set above barely simmering water, stir chocolate until it is almost completely melted. Remove it from heat and stir until it is completely melted. Add oil and stir until chocolate is smooth and glossy.

6. Dip half of each cookie in chocolate and shake off excess. Lay chocolate-dipped cookies on prepared baking sheets to dry completely. Store between layers of parchment paper in an airtight container for up to 1 week.

1 cup (2 sticks) unsalted butter, room temperature
1½ cups confectioners' sugar
1 egg
1 teaspoon pure vanilla extract
2½ cups all-purpose flour
1 teaspoon baking soda
1 teaspoon cream of tartar
2 tablespoons orange-scented geranium petals*
4 ounces good-quality bittersweet chocolate
1 tablespoon vegetable oil

*Feel free to use another flavor of scented geranium or, better yet, bake a range of different flavors in different shapes. Form dough into two flat rounds, refrigerate it for about 30 minutes, and roll it to ¼ inch thick between 2 sheets of plastic wrap. Cut it into shapes with cookie cutters.

If you don't have a double boiler, set a heatproof glass bowl on top of a pot of water. Just make sure the water doesn't touch the bottom of the bowl.

Rose-Scented Geranium Filo Cups

At first glance, this delicate dessert looks simple. But its few ingredients come together in a thoughtful and balanced composition, much like a good haiku. Fill crisp, delicate pastry cups with light, tart geranium pastry cream and fresh raspberries topped with geranium whipped cream, decorated with the petals of a few flowers. *Makes 12 cups.*

1. Preheat oven to 325°F. Brush the insides of a 12-cup muffin pan with butter. Cover filo dough with a barely damp towel and a piece of plastic wrap.

2. Working with one square at a time, brush filo with melted butter and place in muffin cups. Use at least 3 squares of filo per cup. Bake until cups are golden brown, about 6 minutes. Turn cups out of pan and set them right side up for filling.

3. Place a dollop of pastry cream in each cup and top with several fresh berries. On top of that, place a small heap of scented whipped cream and a couple of geranium flowers. Serve.

Pastry cream is a staple in sweet kitchens because it has a million uses. We use ours to fill cakes, doughnuts, tarts, cream puffs, and éclairs. Plain vanilla pastry cream is good, but jazz it up with a little flower sugar, and you've got something great.

6 sheets filo dough, cut into 3-inch squares

3 tablespoons unsalted butter, melted

2 cups mixed fresh raspberries

2 cups scented geranium pastry cream (page 183)

1 cup rose-scented geranium whipped cream (page 183)

Petals of 24 rose-scented geranium flowers (about ½ cup)*

*Rose-scented geranium flowers or any other scented geranium flowers will taste great.

Flower Whipped Cream

A treat with cake or any dessert, flower whipped creams are quick and easy to make. Enhance the flavor by infusing cold cream with scented geranium petals as well as leaves (which are more fragrant). See how on page 182.

Geranium Angel Cake

I grew up in a kosher home, and Shabbat dinner was a ritual my whole family looked forward to. A busy week under our belts, we would all sit at the table sparkling with my mother's finest dishes, light the candles, sip the wine, and let the weekend begin. My mother's angel food cake hanging upside down on a wine bottle was a harbinger of the meal to come. I remember marveling at it perched there, defying gravity until we were ready to run a knife around its edges, carefully put it on a plate, and pounce. Fragrant geranium leaves or petals pressed into the cake bump up the flavor, and you can vary the species for different flavors: roses, lime or lemon, or chocolate mint. *Makes one 9-inch Bundt cake.*

½ cup geranium leaves and/or petals (from about 6 flowers),* divided
1½ cups sugar, divided
1 cup sifted cake flour
12 egg whites (about 1½ cups), room temperature
1 teaspoon cream of tartar
¼ teaspoon salt
1 teaspoon pure vanilla extract

*Use more leaves for a more strongly scented cake. The petals tend to carry much less of a scent.

1. Preheat oven to 325°F. Listen carefully, because this might be the only time you'll ever read this: set aside an *ungreased* Bundt pan. Arrange a few geranium leaves and/or petals at various spots in bottom of pan.

2. Grind 2 tablespoons of the geraniums with ¾ cup of the sugar in the bowl of a food processor. Whisk to combine flour and the remaining ¾ cup sugar in a small bowl.

3. Using a mixer fitted with the whisk attachment, whip egg whites on high speed for about 1 minute, until frothy. Add cream of tartar and salt and keep beating for about 2 minutes more, until whites are foamy. Gradually beat in geranium sugar. Beat until sugar is fully incorporated and whites have turned to soft peaks, about 5 minutes more.

4. Gently fold flour-sugar mixture into whites and, just before it is all combined, gently stir in vanilla. Spoon the batter into Bundt pan and tap pan on the counter two times to pop any large air bubbles.

5. Bake for 50 minutes to 1 hour, or until cake is golden brown and feels springy to the touch. Invert cake on a wire rack or the neck of a glass bottle to cool for at least several hours and up to 24 hours. Run a thin knife around the edge to release it from the pan. Serve immediately or store in an airtight container for up to 3 days.

Processing geraniums with your sugar will accomplish two things: It will release the aromatic essential oils from the flowers into the sugar, and it will grind the sugar to a superfine texture, which is ideal for a light, airy angel cake.

It is the leaf that gives off the most of a geranium's flavor and scent. Use leaves in addition to—or instead of—petals for more potent geranium flavor.

Herb Flowers

Flower Names: Basil, borage, chamomile, chive, lavender, oregano, rosemary, and sage

Botanical Names: *Ocimum basilicum* (basil), *Borago officinalis* (borage), *Matricaria recutita* (German chamomile) and *Anthemis nobilis* (Roman chamomile), *Allium schoenoprasum* (chive), *Lavandula* (lavender), *Origanum vulgare* (oregano), *Rosmarinus officinalis* (rosemary), and *Salvia officinalis* (sage)

Nicknames: king of herbs (basil), starflower (borage), earth apple (chamomile), allium (chive), the pizza herb (oregano), holy herb (rosemary), and healing herb (sage)

Language of Flowers: Herbs signify hate (basil), courage and bluntness (borage), prosperity (chive), joy (oregano), devotion (lavender), remembrance (rosemary), and good health and long life (sage).

Background: The word *basil* comes from the Greek *basileus*, meaning "king," perhaps because the basil flower's mouth is said to resemble a basilisk, the king of all serpents. Ancient warriors drank a tisane (herbal tea) of borage to give them courage before entering battle. And according to an old wives' tale, a man should drink borage to muster the courage to ask for a woman's hand in marriage. One legend has it that lavender received its scent from the baby Jesus, after Mary washed his blanket and hung it to dry on a lavender plant; it appears in the Bible as "spikenard" for Naarda, the Syrian city where it grew. Judith, a Hebrew heroine, anoints herself with lavender before seducing and beheading the general Holofernes and saving Jerusalem. In Greek, *oregano* means "joy of the mountain." The Greek goddess Aphrodite is said to have created the scent of oregano as a symbol of happiness. Pliny the Elder wrote that rosemary was twined into wreaths and worn at weddings to symbolize fidelity and love. A pot of rosemary placed by the door is said to keep witches at bay. Sage's name (salvia) comes from the Latin *salvere*, "to be saved."

Culinary Use: Herb flowers are an ideal replacement for the leaves when a more delicate taste is desired. Subtly peppery and sweet with an underlying menthol taste, fresh basil is commonly found in Italian and Asian cooking. Borage's cucumber flavors are delicious in salads and garnishes, and the leaves can be steamed and eaten like spinach. Chive has a mild onion-garlic flavor perfect for salads and vinegars. Lavender is used in France for desserts, vinegars, and the herb blend *herbes de Provence*. Rosemary is woody with a hint of mint. Aromatic, warm, and slightly bitter, oregano is used in Italian cuisine and to flavor meat in Turkish cooking. Piney and pungent, rosemary stems are sometimes used as skewers for meat or poultry. It is used in roasted meats and vegetables and is especially well suited to game. Savory and assertive, sage enhances meat, pork, and starches.

Seasonality: Blooming in early spring through summer's end, herb flowers can be dried for use all year long. They are easy to grow, and many reseed themselves each year. If you plant your herbs in pots a bit too small, the flowers will arrive much sooner.

Preparation: Herb flowers and buds come away easily from their stems. I find the best method is to run my hand backward along the stem and push the flowers off. Oregano offers its flowers in umbels to be cut off. Chive flowers can be plucked from their flowerhead between thumb and forefinger, but don't forget to eat the tasty green stem.

Measure: 1 cup herb flowers = 50 to 100 flowers (used whole but without stems and leaves).

Herb Flower Pesto

This fantastic pesto combines the complex flavors of various herb flowers—use whatever you have on hand. After the herbs bloom but before they set seed, grab some blossoms and grind them up. You can use this pesto on pasta or bruschetta, but it also makes a great topping for fish or marinade for poultry, beef, or pork. *Makes 2 cups.*

Pulse nuts, herb flowers, garlic, and salt in the bowl of a food processor. Whir in olive oil and Parmesan, if using.

Putting Up Pesto

If you want to store a bit of summer in a jar, put this pesto in your freezer and pull it out when you are most coveting spicy sunny days. I freeze mine in an ice cube tray and then transfer the frozen cubes to freezer bags so I can use a bit at a time.

Herb flowers are often looked at with distaste by chefs and gardeners because their appearance signifies that the herb is getting bitter. But the blossoms have wonderful flavors all their own. Oregano, sage, and rosemary flowers have a milder flavor than the leaves, making them ideal for baking. Chive blossoms impart a spicy, oniony flavor that's perfect for use in salads and vinegars. Try thyme, savory, mint, fennel, lemon verbena, cilantro, monarda, chervil, garlic, and anise hyssop flowers; a mix of fresh herb flowers will complement almost any recipe.

¾ cup pine nuts or walnuts, toasted*
3½ cups herb flowers such as basil, sage, and rosemary**
4 cloves garlic, peeled and chopped
½ teaspoon salt
½ cup extra-virgin olive oil
¼ cup Parmesan cheese, grated (optional)

*Spread nuts on a baking sheet and toast them in a 350°F oven—tossing occasionally, for a consistent color—for about 8 minutes, or until they start to turn golden brown and release a strong nutty scent.

**Fennel, lemon balm, and marjoram flowers also make good pesto.

Herb Flower Shortbread

I love using savory ingredients in traditionally sweet recipes and working sweet ingredients into traditionally savory recipes. This shortbread is one of those wonderful sweet-yet-savory treats. Is it a cookie? An addition to your cheese plate? An appetizer? Maybe all three. *Makes one 9-inch square pan.*

1¾ cups all-purpose flour
½ cup rice flour
1 cup (2 sticks) unsalted butter, room temperature
½ cup sugar
¾ teaspoon flaky sea salt (such as Maldon)
1 tablespoon lemon zest
4 tablespoon herb flowers (whatever you have on hand)

1. Preheat oven to 350°F. Line a 9-inch square pan with foil and put a square of parchment on the bottom.

It might seem redundant to use both foil and parchment to line the pan, but for this recipe it makes good sense if you want to "double-bake" it in step 4.

2. Sift flours together twice. Beat butter with a mixer on medium speed for at least 3 minutes, until light and creamy. Slowly add sugar with the mixer on low speed. Scrape down the sides of the bowl to make sure it's all in.

3. Stir salt, lemon zest, and herb flowers into flour mixture. Gently work flour into butter mixture, being careful not to overmix. (This ensures light, buttery shortbread.)

4. Press batter into the prepared pan and bake for about 50 minutes, or until the top is golden brown. At this point you can let it cool, slice it, and serve. Or, for a crisp, crunchy shortbread, let it cool for about 10 minutes, slice it into 1½-by-2-inch rectangles (which leaves a little left over for the chef to nibble on), spread it out on a foil-lined baking sheet, and put it back in the oven for 10 minutes to brown the edges.

Blackberry Borage Fool

A fool is a simple, old-fashioned English dessert made with fruit folded into whipped cream. It is so light you could fool yourself into thinking it has no calories at all, and the layers of flavors are complex enough that it is satisfying without being filling. British accent is optional. *Serves 4.*

1. Put heavy cream and borage flowers in a covered container and refrigerate for at least 2 hours and up to 24 hours. In a bowl, combine 2 cups of the blackberries with lime juice and ginger and let them infuse for the same amount of time as the cream.

2. Mash the blackberry mixture by hand or in a food processor.

3. Strain borage-infused cream through a fine-mesh strainer and discard the solids. Combine with confectioners' sugar in the bowl of a mixer, and whip on medium-high speed for 5 minutes, or until cream is soft and billowy, but firm. Reserve a small amount for garnish, if desired.

4. Gently fold blackberry mash into borage cream. Divide the remaining 2 cups of blackberries between four tall cups or parfait glasses and top with the borage blackberry cream. Garnish with reserved borage cream, if desired, and borage flowers.

1 cup heavy cream

⅓ cup borage flowers, plus extra for garnish

4 cups fresh blackberries, divided

1 tablespoon freshly squeezed lime juice

1 teaspoon freshly grated ginger (from about ½ inch fresh ginger root)

1 tablespoon confectioners' sugar

To use borage flowers, first pluck the flower from the plant at the base of its stem. Then wash and dry the flowers and, using a thumb and forefinger, gently tug at one of the five blue petals. The blue flower should easily come apart from its hairy green star-shaped receptacle.

Borage Spritzer

Borage spritzer is so refreshing on a hot summer night, after dinner with dear friends when you want a little something to cool you down and pick you up. *Serves 4.*

Combine syrup, vodka, and seltzer in a big pitcher and stir well. Fill each of four glasses with borage ice cubes and pour the spritzer over top. Garnish each glass with cucumber and basil. Kick off your shoes and drink up.

½ cup borage basil simple syrup
  (page 177)
½ cup borage vodka (page 180)
3 cups seltzer water
Borage ice cubes*
8 cucumber slices
8 basil leaves

*Borage ice cubes are beautiful, glittering, shimmering pieces of ice with cobalt blue blossoms twinkling inside. For how to make them, see page 180.

Borage Basil Lemonade
Not in the mood for alcohol, or have children around who need their own grown-up-looking summer specialty drink? Replace the vodka with lemon juice and you've got a perfect substitute.

Crème Fraîche Chamomile Ice Cream

The slightly apple-y flavor of chamomile works so well with the tang of crème fraîche. Try this plain, then try it with peaches grilled or roasted with fresh rosemary. You will not regret it, you will want to repeat it, and you will make a lot of friends! *Makes 1 quart.*

Toss everything into a blender and blend for about 3 minutes, or until mixture has the smooth, creamy texture of a thin milkshake; occasionally scrape down the sides of the blender to make sure all ingredients are incorporated. Chill the mixture until very cold, about 1 hour if you started with very cold ingredients. Process the chilled mixture in an ice-cream machine according to manufacturer's instructions.

Know Your Chamomile

Roman vs. German chamomile: what's the difference? The two types are closely related. They can be used interchangeably, though many people have a favorite. Roman chamomile has a flattened head, whereas German is more dome shaped. Roman chamomile is used as a ground cover and doesn't grow taller than one foot; German chamomile can grow 2 to 3 feet tall.

About 2 cups (1 pound) very cold crème fraîche*
1¾ cups very cold whole milk
¼ cup very cold heavy cream
½ cup strong chamomile tea (page 181), room temperature
1 cup sugar

*Crème fraîche is a thick cultured cream with a rich texture and slightly tangy flavor.

Crème Fraîche

Combine 2 cups heavy cream with 2 tablespoons buttermilk in a clean glass jar. Shake to mix and let it sit at room temperature for 12 to 24 hours, until mixture thickens and has a texture like that of sour cream. Use it or store it, covered, in the refrigerator for up to 1 week.

Don't have the time—or the buttermilk—to make crème fraîche? Simply subsitute full-fat Greek yogurt or sour cream.

Popcorn-Chive Blossom Cupcakes

Popcorn and chives in a cupcake? Trust me, you'll love the play on sweet and savory. These dainty cups are filled with just enough flowers to make people wonder, and the popcorn flavor works so well with the butter cake. *Makes 12 cupcakes.*

1. Soak popcorn in milk for about 2 hours. (If you want to leave it longer, refrigerate it, but bring it back to room temperature before you use it.)

2. Strain popcorn through a fine-mesh strainer, pressing the soggy popcorn to get all the good stuff out. Discard the solids.

3. Preheat oven to 350°F and line a 12-cup cupcake or muffin pan with liners.

4. Put flour, sugar, baking powder, salt, and chive petals in the bowl of a mixer and mix briefly to combine. Add 1¼ cups of the strained popcorn milk and butter to flour mixture and beat for about 2 minutes on medium-low speed.

5. Drop egg yolks and vanilla into the remaining ¾ cup strained popcorn milk and mix with a fork to break up yolks. Beat mixture into the batter a bit at a time, pausing occasionally to scrape down the sides of the mixing bowl.

6. Fill the muffin cups two-thirds with batter and slide the pan into the oven. Bake cupcakes for about 20 minutes, or until a toothpick inserted into the center of one comes out clean. Let cool on a wire rack.

7. For the frosting, beat cream cheese, butter, confectioners' sugar, and vanilla with a mixer on medium speed for 3 to 5 minutes, or until no lumps remain. Frost each cupcake and top with chive blossom petals, if desired. Serve the same day.

   Be careful not to overbeat the frosting or it'll be forever liquidy and won't hold nice peaks. Better to underbeat, check for lumps, and continue—or frost the cupcakes.

CUPCAKES

2 cups popped popcorn

2 cups milk

2½ cups all-purpose flour, sifted

1½ cups sugar

1 tablespoon plus 1 teaspoon baking powder

¾ teaspoon salt

Petals of 4 chive blossoms, plus more for topping, if desired

¾ cup (1½ sticks) unsalted butter, room temperature

6 large egg yolks

1 tablespoon pure vanilla extract

FROSTING

1 (8-ounce) package cream cheese

3 tablespoons unsalted butter, room temperature

2½ cups confectioners' sugar

1 teaspoon pure vanilla extract

Lavender Mango Sandwich Cookies

These shortbreads are delicate. When I say delicate, I mean they do not stand up well to shipping, so if you were thinking of sending them to friends, invite them over instead. Lavender shortbread is the perfect accompaniment for tart, sweet mango buttercream (recipe opposite) or mango conserves of any kind. *Makes about 24 sandwiches.*

1. Combine flour and salt in a bowl; set aside.

2. With a mixer, beat butter and sugar on low speed for about 1 minute and then, over the course of another minute, increase the speed gradually and beat until mixture is light and fluffy; when you reach high speed, beat it for 5 minutes more. Mix in egg yolks, one at a time, making sure each one is fully incorporated before adding the next. Add vanilla and lavender and then beat mixture on medium speed for 2 minutes to help lavender release its essential oils into butter. Add flour mixture and beat until you don't see any streaks of flour.

3. Lay a large (14-by-18-inch) sheet of parchment paper on the counter and scoop the ridiculously soft and messy dough right onto it, forming a log that's 2 inches in diameter and about 16 inches long. This can get messy; if you are a perfectionist like me and want it to be nice and even, you may need to refrigerate the dough for about 30 minutes before smoothing out the log. Refrigerate the rolled log for at least 2 hours and up to overnight, or freeze it for up to 2 months. (I like to slice and bake mine straight out of the freezer.)

4. Preheat oven to 350°F and line baking sheets with parchment paper. Cut dough log into ¼-inch-thick slices and place them about 1 inch apart on prepared baking sheets. Sprinkle the top of each cookie with a touch of sugar. Bake cookies for about 10 minutes, or until just golden brown around the edges. Let them cool on their baking sheets.

5. Flip half of the cooled cookies upside down and spread a little mango buttercream (or conserve) on the upturned halves. Sandwich with unspread cookies and voilà! Sandwiched cookies should be eaten within a few hours, but you may store the unfilled cookies for up to 4 days in an airtight container.

3 cups all-purpose flour

1 teaspoon salt

1½ cups (3 sticks) unsalted butter, room temperature

1 cup sugar,* plus about 2 tablespoons for sprinkling

6 egg yolks

1 teaspoon pure vanilla extract

1 tablespoon dried lavender buds or 4 tablespoons fresh lavender buds

½ cup mango buttercream (opposite) or mango conserves

*It's a good time to use lavender sugar (page 176). It isn't essential, but it adds a lovely flavor.

For these cookies, it is not so important to get the butter and sugar light and fluffy; just beat enough to make sure they are well combined.

Mango Buttercream

½ cup (1 stick) unsalted butter,
    room temperature
1 mango, peeled, sliced, and mashed
1 teaspoon lime juice
3 cups confectioners' sugar, more or
    less to taste

Beat butter until smooth. Add
mango and lime juice and beat for
about 3 minutes. Beat in confectioners' sugar, a bit at a time. You
might not need the whole amount
of sugar or you might opt for more,
depending on the consistency and
flavor you are looking for. Makes
about 2 cups.

Lavender Cookies Topped with Berries Dipped in White Chocolate

I sometimes feel lazy and dispense
with the whole sandwich-cookie
production. Try skipping the mango
buttercream and instead dip fresh
berries in melted white chocolate.
Perch one in the center of each
cookie, and you'll have a pretty
dessert-table treat in no time.

Chocolate Lavender Biscotti

My husband, Noah, always says that biscotti are just stale cookies, but I couldn't disagree more. Biscotti are crispy, airy, crumbly, and delicious. This recipe is so flavorful—with its combination of chocolate, hazelnut, and lavender—that you might forget it contains no butter. *Makes about 30.*

1. In a large bowl combine flour, cocoa powder, sugar, lavender buds, baking soda, and salt. Make a well in the center of dry ingredients. Add eggs and vanilla in the center and mix everything together by hand. Mix in hazelnuts and chocolate. The resulting dough should be sticky.

2. Cut 2 sheets of parchment paper at least 12 by 18 inches. Place half the dough on one sheet and half on the other and form the dough into two 14-inch logs. Wrap logs in parchment and refrigerate for 2 hours or up to overnight.

3. Preheat oven to 350°F. Unroll dough logs and transfer them to parchment-lined baking sheets. Bake for about 25 minutes. Remove pans from the oven and reduce the oven temperature to 300°F. With a serrated knife, slice logs as you would a loaf of bread, either straight across or on the diagonal, into slices about ¹/₂ inch thick.

4. Line the baking sheets with fresh parchment paper and place sliced biscotti on top. I like to try to stand my slices up vertically and keep them about ¹/₄ inch apart so that air can circulate around them, but if yours will not stand up, lay them on their sides. Bake for 25 minutes more; if your biscotti are lying down, flip them over about 15 minutes in. Let biscotti cool to room temperature on a wire rack. Store biscotti for up to 2 weeks in an airtight tin.

Pineapple Sage Biscotti
Replace lavender buds with 5 tablespoons pineapple sage flowers.

Rose Petal Biscotti
Replace lavender buds with 5 tablespoons rose petals.

2 cups all-purpose flour
¾ cup cocoa powder
1¼ cups sugar
2 tablespoons lavender buds
1 teaspoon baking soda
¼ teaspoon salt
4 eggs
1 teaspoon pure vanilla extract
1 cup hazelnuts, lightly toasted*
¾ cup (1½ ounces) roughly chopped milk chocolate

*Spread nuts on a baking sheet and toast them in a 350°F oven, tossing occasionally, for about 8 minutes, or until they start to turn golden brown and release a strong nutty aroma.

Biscotti store well in cookie tins—up to 2 weeks—and make great gifts.

Lavender Lemon Blackberry Pound Cake

The combination of lavender, blackberry, and lemon makes this lovely cake lightly sweet and tart. Though I like pound cake as an ending to a summer supper, I have been known to sneak a piece and toast it for breakfast, turning it into "French cake" for my son Ijie. *Makes one 9-by-5-by-3-inch loaf or 12 mini cakes.*

1. Preheat oven to 325°F. If you are using a single loaf pan, coat it with nonstick spray. If you are using disposable mini loaf pans, set them on a baking sheet.

2. Submerge lavender buds in buttermilk and let them infuse for 30 minutes or longer. (If you aren't going to make the cakes within the next 2 hours, cover and refrigerate the infusion until you're ready to bake.)

3. Sift together flour, baking powder, and salt in a bowl. Add blackberries and toss until they're thoroughly coated. (Coating berries in the flour mixture prevents them from sinking to the bottom of the batter.)

4. Beat butter with a mixer on medium speed for 2 minutes, or until smooth and creamy. Gradually beat in sugar. Beat mixture for 5 minutes, or until it is once again light and fluffy. Stop mixer and scrape down the sides of the bowl. Beat in eggs, one at a time, and make sure they don't just sit at the bottom of the mixing bowl. Mix in lemon zest and juice. Turn off mixer and do the rest of the mixing by hand, first stirring in some of the flour mixture, then the lavender-buttermilk infusion, and finally the remaining flour mixture.

5. Pour cake batter into the prepared pan(s) and bake for 35 to 40 minutes for a single pound cake or 25 to 30 minutes for mini cakes. The top of the cake will be golden and a metal tester inserted in the center will come out clean. Let it rest in the pan for about 5 minutes before flipping it out onto a wire rack to finish cooling. Pour glaze over cake and eat it right away or store it for up to 4 days wrapped in an airtight container.

4 tablespoons fresh lavender buds
   (or 2 tablespoons dried)
¾ cup buttermilk
2½ cups sifted all-purpose flour
1½ teaspoons baking powder
½ teaspoon salt
1 pint blackberries
1 cup (2 sticks) unsalted butter,
   room temperature
2 cups sugar
4 eggs plus 2 egg yolks
Zest of 1 lemon
2 tablespoons lemon juice

Lemon Glaze

2 cups confectioners' sugar
3 tablespoons lemon juice

Whisk confectioners' sugar and lemon juice until no lumps remain.

For glaze that melts into pound cake and virtually disappears, you'll want to mix the glaze together quickly and pour it on as soon as the cake is done baking. For a thicker glaze, wait 20 minutes or until the cake is no longer hot, but not quite room temperature either, before glazing it.

Lavender Blueberry Earl Grey Pound Cake

Lavender and blueberries work remarkably well with Earl Grey tea. Change the flavor of this pound cake by replacing the lemon zest and juice with a bag of Earl Grey tea leaves. Open up the bag and dump tea leaves into batter. Swap in blueberries instead of blackberries.

Caramelized Peaches with Lavender Cream

Peaches. The very word makes my mouth water. Peaches and cream is even better, but toss a little lavender in the mix and this dessert becomes truly special. Aromatic lavender cream grounds the flavor of heady sweet peaches, and the whole composition is so versatile you could serve it at a formal dinner with a glass of dessert wine or bring it to a backyard barbecue. Either way, you won't hear complaints. *Serves 6.*

¼ cup (½ stick) unsalted butter, room temperature

¾ cup sugar

6 mint leaves

1½ teaspoons lavender buds (from 2 sprigs)

6 peaches, halved and pitted

2 cups lavender simple syrup (page 177) or lavender whipped cream (page 183), for topping

1. Preheat oven to 400°F. Line a baking sheet with parchment paper.

2. Smash butter, sugar, mint leaves, and lavender buds together with a fork, mashing well. Spread the cut side of each peach half with butter mixture. Place peaches cut side down on the prepared baking sheet. Bake for about 20 minutes, or until they are semisoft and yield easily to a fork. Arrange peaches cut side up in serving bowls. Top with lavender simple syrup or lavender whipped cream.

Lavender Lemonade

Delightfully refreshing, lavender lemonade is a great way to showcase your skill at making flower simple syrups. *Makes 6 cups (1½ quarts).*

Mix ingredients directly in the pitcher—don't bother dirtying up one more thing. Adjust the flavors according to your own taste preferences.

1 cup lavender simple syrup (page 177)
1 cup lemon juice
4 cups water

See page 76 for borage spritzer and borage basil lemonade; page 185 for lilac lemonade, sparkling geranium limeade, hibiscus basil watermelonade, and more.

Rosemary Flower Margaritas

I say this recipe serves four, but that really depends on how "thirsty" you are. I love a good margarita; they remind me of summer and backyard parties. A little savory herbal woodiness is a perfect addition, thanks to the rosemary flowers. At the Mali B confectionery shop, we combine passionfruit with rosemary in several of our desserts; it's an excellent combination in a cocktail as well. *Serves 4.*

Combine tequila with rosemary flowers and let sit for at least 2 weeks; the longer the rosemary sits in the tequila, the more pronounced its flavor will be. Strain rosemary-infused tequila, discarding the solids, into a cocktail shaker and add passionfruit puree, Cointreau, and rosemary simple syrup. Shake well and strain into glasses filled with crushed ice. .

Don't have 2 weeks? Double the amount of rosemary and infuse the tequila for just 1 week.

Flower Margaritas
Other flower margarita combinations to try are pineapple and basil, hibiscus and pomegranate, and nasturtium and orange.

1 cup tequila
¼ cup rosemary flowers
½ cup passionfruit puree*
¼ cup Cointreau or other orange-flavored liqueur
1 tablespoon rosemary simple syrup (page 177)
Crushed ice

*The combination of passionfruit and rosemary is heavenly! That said, passionfruit puree can be a little tricky to find. You can substitute mango puree or pineapple juice.

Rosemary Flower Madeleines

Dainty, shell-shaped French madeleines were made famous when Marcel Proust waxed poetic about them in *Swann's Way*, using them as a metaphor for involuntary memories that sneak up and grab you unbidden. Rosemary flowers enhance the madeleines' delicate aroma. They're a fitting addition, because rosemary has been considered a symbol of remembrance since Shakespeare's time. *Makes 24 cookies.*

1 cup (2 sticks) unsalted butter, divided
4 eggs
⅔ cup sugar
¾ cup all-purpose flour
2 tablespoons finely ground cornmeal
1 teaspoon baking powder
¼ teaspoon salt
¼ to ⅓ cup rosemary flowers
Zest of 1 lemon
1 teaspoon pure vanilla extract

1. Put butter in a small saucepan over low heat and cook, swirling the pan occasionally, for about 15 minutes, or until butter begins to brown and gives off a nutty aroma.

   Watch browning butter carefully; it can quickly turn black.

2. In the bowl of a mixer fitted with the whisk attachment, beat the eggs on high speed for about 10 minutes, or until they triple in volume and turn pale yellow. Gradually beat in sugar, watching for the mixture to become paler and grow a bit more in volume.

3. Combine flour, cornmeal, baking powder, and salt in a bowl. Gently fold flour mixture, rosemary flowers, lemon zest, and vanilla into whipped eggs. Drizzle all but about 2 tablespoons of the brown butter into the batter and fold again. Scoop batter into an airtight quart container and let it rest in the refrigerator for about 4 hours.

   Chilling and resting the batter is key to achieving the signature humps on the tops of the madeleines.

4. Preheat oven to 400°F. Brush the wells of a madeleine pan with the reserved 2 tablespoons brown butter, or take a shortcut and coat them with nonstick spray. Spoon batter into pan. Bake for about 15 minutes. When the humps have risen and the edges begin to take on a bit of a golden tinge, reduce the oven temperature to 375°F and bake for about 5 minutes more, or until the edges are deep golden. Madeleines are best eaten the day they are made, but they can be stored in a tin for a couple of days.

Hibiscus and Hollyhocks

Botanical Name: *Hibiscus rosa-sinensis* and *Alcea*

Nicknames: False roselle and shoe flower (hibiscus); St. Joseph's staff, hock leaf, and dancing ladies (hollyhock)

Language of Flowers: Hibiscus stands for delicate beauty, and hollyhock for fertility and fruitfulness.

Background: Hibiscus is a member of the mallow family, one that in Greek mythology was considered the first messenger sent to earth to express the sympathy the gods felt for the short lives of mortals. In some Pacific island cultures, hibiscus helps identify a woman's intentions: if she wears a hibiscus behind her right ear, she is spoken for or wishes to remain chaste; behind the left, she is available for love; and behind both, she is open to more than one romantic partner! Hibiscus petals are used to shine shoes in India and other parts of the world, earning them names that translate as "shoe flowers."

Hollyhocks take their name from "holy" and "mallow" (*hoc,* meaning "mallow" in Old English) and were imported from China to Britain by the Crusaders. Hollyhock remains were among the herbs found in a fifty-thousand-year-old gravesite.

Culinary Use: Hibiscus has a slight tang, but its flavor is mild. Today it is commonly used in salads and alcoholic beverages, and the dried or candied flowers are becoming popular. Hollyhock flowers are also mildly flavored and traditionally used in salads. Both hibiscus and hollyhocks are members of the mallow family. Another member of the mallow family known as marsh mallow (*Althea sinensis*) was once prized for its mucilaginous roots, which ancient Egyptians used to make fluffy, sticky candy. Today there are much easier ways to make marshmallows without using real mallows (see page 56).

Seasonality: Hibiscus blooms in summer. In warm climates, it can be grown outdoors as a perennial; in other areas, it can be left outside in summer and brought indoors during winter.

Hollyhock flowers in early summer to midsummer. It runs amok in many gardens, but if that's not the case in yours, you may want to visit your local garden center or nursery to purchase some. The flowers are not available commercially because they do not last more than a day once picked.

Preparation: Remove hibiscus flowers from the plant at its base. Pull the pistil (with the stamens attached) from the center of the flower and pluck off the individual petals. To substitute dried hibiscus for fresh, triple the amount. To rehydrate dried hibiscus, cover the flowers with warm water and let soak until they have plumped, 10 to 15 minutes. To prepare hollyhock flowers, wash and dry them before clutching the calyx (the green bottom part) and pulling the petals away from the pistil.

Measure: 1 cup hibiscus or hollyhock petals = petals from 6 to 12 flowers.

Hibiscus Fried Rice

Lots of vegetarians have to suffer through bad takeout versions of vegetarian fried rice. This recipe is easy to make and inspiring to taste, and I guarantee it'll make you a star in your favorite vegetarian's eyes. *Serves 4.*

1. In a small bowl, whisk eggs with hibiscus powder, salt, and pepper.

2. Heat a wok or a large, heavy-bottom pan over high heat. Add about 1 tablespoon of the oil and swirl it around to coat the pan. Add onion. When it warms up and begins to sweat, add ginger, scallion whites, and garlic (if using). Stir everything together for just less than 1 minute and then transfer it all to a large serving dish.

3. With the pan emptied and back on the heat, add 2 more tablespoons of the oil and swirl it around to coat the pan. Cook egg mixture, stirring to ensure that it doesn't turn into an omelette (that's for another time), but rather scrambled eggs. Flip the eggs on to the onion mix and return pan to heat.

4. Warm the remaining 1 tablespoon of oil. Add rice and stir with a wooden spoon to break it up and coat with oil. Return everything from the serving dish to the pan and toss briefly with rice. Transfer it all to the serving dish and add chopped hibiscus flowers. Serve hot.

Why keep hibiscus powder around? Lots of reasons! It makes a tart, tangy tea (1 tablespoon per cup boiling water), and it can be used in applesauce or any rhubarb recipe. Mix it into strawberry or raspberry jam to deepen the red color and add a little flavor. Or stir a spoonful into lemonade and voilà—pink lemonade. In fact, hibiscus powder complements all kinds of cocktails, from margaritas to martinis.

3 eggs
1 teaspoon hibiscus powder*
½ teaspoon salt
Freshly ground pepper, to taste
4 tablespoons vegetable oil, divided**
1 onion, diced
1 (2-inch) piece fresh ginger, peeled and chopped
2 scallions, sliced into thin rings, whites and greens separated
3 cloves garlic, finely chopped (optional)
4 cups cold cooked rice
½ cup hibiscus flowers, chopped

*Hibiscus powder is ground dried hibiscus flowers. You can make your own with blossoms you've dried or grind dried hibiscus you've purchased (see "Sources," page 186).

**I particularly like grapeseed oil, but any vegetable oil will do.

Hibiscus Chutney

Warm, spicy, and rarely sweet—even when it's made with sweet ingredients—chutney is altogether satisfying as a condiment but versatile enough to be used on proteins or even a cheese plate. Delicate hibiscus flowers pair well with blackberries, and they are typically in season around the same time. *Makes 1 pint.*

Toss everything except vinegar into a big pot. Cook and occasionally stir the mixture over medium heat for about 5 minutes. Add salt and pepper if you wish. Stir in vinegar and let mixture simmer and thicken for about 10 minutes more. Refrigerated in an airtight container, this chutney will last for up to 6 weeks.

2 pints fresh blackberries
  (or 1 pound frozen)
8 hibiscus flowers
½ cup red onion, finely chopped
½ cup sugar
1 jalapeño pepper, seeded and
  chopped
2 tablespoons minced fresh ginger
2 tablespoons Dijon mustard
Salt and pepper to taste (optional)
½ cup white wine vinegar

Hibiscus Popsicles

My friend Joe introduced me to the simple delight that is hibiscus in champagne. He dropped a candied hibiscus into the bottom of my glass, and I was head over heels. You've got to try Joe's drink in pop form—it's the best of both worlds. *Makes 10 to 12 popsicles, depending on mold size.*

Stir together simple syrup and champagne. Let stand until mixture stops fizzing. Pour into pop molds and freeze.

2 cups hibiscus simple syrup
   (page 177)
2 cups champagne

Hibiscus Champagne

Store-bought candied hibiscus are destined for bubbly. Drop them into glasses of cool champagne and drink up!

Hibiscus Chili Caramel

Homemade caramel sauce makes you a rock star. Seriously, dispense with the store-bought and make your own. My dear friend Lizz told me one day that she dreamed of roasted chili pepper dipped in caramel. This is my take on her dream: tart and bright hibiscus tea and smoky cayenne pepper turned into a caramel sauce. Swirl it into ice cream, bake it into pie, poach pears in it, fold it into buttercream frosting, or ribbon it in brownies. There are so many ways you can use this delight. *Makes 1 pint.*

3 cups boiling water
1 cup dried hibiscus flowers
1 tablespoon cayenne pepper
1 cup sugar
⅓ cup light corn syrup
1 tablespoon milk chocolate, roughly chopped
5 tablespoons unsalted butter

1. Pour boiling water over hibiscus flowers. Let stand for 15 minutes before straining and reserve 1⅓ cups of the hibiscus infusion in a bowl. Stir in cayenne and let it steep.

2. Put sugar in a clean, dry saucepan over medium heat and cook, stirring, until it melts and turns golden brown; be careful not to let it burn. Pour hibiscus chili tea over caramelized sugar, being careful because the mixture may sizzle and pop (and hot sugar hurts). Stir in corn syrup and cook, stirring occasionally, until temperature reaches 220°F on a candy thermometer. Remove from heat.

3. Let mixture cool but leave the candy thermometer in the caramel because you still need to check temperatures. When the temperature is 90°F whisk in butter, making sure any butter that settles around the edges gets whisked into the caramel. Add chocolate and stir to combine.

4. Transfer caramel to a clean jar and cap it. It will keep in the refrigerator for up to 6 months or at room temperature for up to 6 weeks.

Hibiscus Cream Pie

At Mali B we frequently get asked to make confections featuring ombré designs, or slight gradations of color. Packing that into a pie seemed like a challenge, but we achieved it with hibiscus cream pie. Noticeable flecks of hibiscus run through the crust and custard; the color variations in the cream are subtle, but they're enough to make that gradation change that pleases the eye, and the tart hibiscus sure does please the palate. *Makes one 9-inch pie.*

1. Combine flours, salt, and hibiscus sugar (if using) in the bowl of a food processor and whir for about 30 seconds or 5 pulses. Or, if you don't have a food processor, whisk these ingredients together by hand.

2. Add butter and cream cheese and pulse until they look like big fat peas coated in the flour mixture. Mix in water, a bit at a time, stopping when the mixture just begins to look like dough. Turn it out onto the counter.

3. With the heel of your hand, push down on the dough and away from your body. Fold it back on itself and do it again. Continue the process until the dough comes together but you can still see some streaks of butter and cream cheese. Press dough into a flat disk, cover in plastic wrap, and refrigerate for at least 2 hours.

4. Use a rolling pin to flatten the chilled dough into a 14-inch circle. Transfer it to a pie plate and make certain it is seated properly, without tears. Fold dough under itself to make a proper edge, and crimp it with your fingers or a fork. Cover with plastic wrap and refrigerate again.

5. Preheat oven to 350°F. Weight the chilled crust with pie weights or pennies on parchment paper. Bake until crust is just beginning to brown; remove weights and continue to cook until crust is golden brown throughout, 15 to 18 minutes in all. Let cool.

6. Fill crust with hibiscus pastry cream. Cover pie with plastic wrap and let it cool in the refrigerator or on the counter. When you are an hour or less from serving, top pie with whipped cream.

HIBISCUS PIE CRUST

2 cups all-purpose flour

½ cup pastry flour

1 teaspoon salt

1 teaspoon hibiscus sugar (optional)

¾ cup (1½ sticks) cold unsalted butter, cubed

¼ cup (¼ of an 8-ounce package) cold cream cheese, cubed

About ¼ cup ice water

CREAM FILLING

4 cups hibiscus pastry cream (page 183)

3 generous cups hibiscus whipped cream (page 183)

Flower Pies

You can replace hibiscus with other flowers in both the pie crust and the cream filling. Pansy cream pies and violet cream pies are two of my favorites.

Hollyhock Scones

These light scones have a tart delicacy thanks to a bit of passion-fruit puree and fresh hollyhock petals. Try freezing these lovelies before you bake them and pull them out in winter when you need a hit of sunshine. *Makes 8 scones.*

1. Preheat oven to 400°F. Line a baking sheet with parchment paper or a silicone baking mat.

2. Pulse flour, baking powder, baking soda, salt, and sugar in the bowl of a food processor. Drop in butter and pulse 2 or 3 times, until butter is in pea-size pieces.

3. In a medium bowl whisk eggs, 1/3 cup heavy cream, and passionfruit puree for 2 minutes, or until mixture is a smooth pale yellow. Add to flour mixture, pulsing 2 or 3 times to combine the ingredients and moisten the flour. Just as the mix is threatening to turn into a ball, add hollyhock petals and pulse 3 more times.

4. Spread a little flour on a cutting board and turn the dough onto it. Working carefully—you don't want to manhandle the dough—form it into a 1/2-inch-thick rectangle. You have your choice of how to cut your scones: some people like to stamp out circles with cookie cutters; others slice the dough into rectangles with a knife or a pizza cutter. You can't go wrong either way.

5. Place scones on the prepared baking sheet about 1 inch apart and brush the tops with the remaining 2 tablespoons heavy cream. Bake scones for about 20 minutes, or until golden brown on top. Plate and serve hot with the toppings of your choice.

2½ cups all-purpose flour
2 teaspoons baking powder
1 teaspoon baking soda
Pinch salt
4 tablespoons sugar
5 tablespoons cold unsalted
    butter, cubed
2 eggs
1/3 cup plus 2 tablespoons heavy
    cream, divided
1/4 cup passionfruit puree*
Petals of 6 hollyhock flowers
Butter, honey, and jam or other
    toppings, to serve

*Tangy and slightly acidic, with a sweet edge, passionfruit puree is thick and delicious. Strawberry puree can substitute in a pinch.

Hollyhock Cream Puffs

This one's for my sister-in-law Holly, aunt extraordinaire. She grew up in Iowa and reminisces often about her childhood there, where the hollyhocks grew all around her home. Holly now lives in Arizona, but she still grows hollyhocks. *Makes 24 small or 12 large puffs.*

1. Preheat oven to 425°F. Line 2 baking sheets with parchment paper.

2. In a medium saucepan, bring water and butter to a quick simmer. Get your stirring arm ready and grab a wooden spoon or your favorite mixing utensil. Add flour and beat the heck out of the mixture for about 3 minutes. You will see it come together and pull off the side of the saucepan.

3. Quickly transfer flour mixture to a mixer or food processor and give your arm a rest by letting the machine do the work for another 30 seconds. Add salt and eggs, one at a time, and let the machine work the dough until it is thick, slick, and slippery.

4. Drop spoonfuls of dough onto the prepared baking sheets 2 inches apart. Bake for 10 minutes, then lower temperature to 350°F and bake for another 20 minutes, until puffs are golden brown and hollow sounding when tapped.

   If you choose to, you may form the puffs using a pastry bag for more even rounds. If you end up with peaks, press them down with a wet finger. If the puffs have peaks, they will burn.

5. Place chocolate in a food processor. In a small saucepan over high heat, bring cream to a rapid boil. With the processor running, pour hot cream over chocolate. Process 1 minute more until smooth. Let the resulting ganache rest for 2 minutes before spooning it over cream puffs.

Here's the wonderful thing about cream puffs: they don't mind waiting for you. You can eat them right away or freeze them in an airtight container, filling and serving them later.

CREAM PUFFS

1 cup water
½ cup (1 stick) unsalted butter
1 cup all-purpose flour
1 teaspoon hollyhock sugar (page 176)
Pinch salt
4 eggs

FILLING

About 3 cups hollyhock pastry cream (page 183)

GANACHE

¾ cup heavy cream
1½ cups (9 ounces) semisweet chocolate

Hollyhock Clafouti

Clafouti is a humble French confection that's a cross between a custard, a pancake, and a puffy omelet. It comes together in minutes and is incredibly versatile. You simply pour the batter over cherries or any kind of fruit, stone or otherwise. I have had great luck with plums. *Serves 6, or a few hungry teenagers.*

½ cup milk
½ cup heavy cream
4 eggs
1 teaspoon pure vanilla extract
½ cup sugar
¼ cup all-purpose flour
Pinch salt
2 cups cherries
1 cup hollyhock petals (from about 4 to 6 flowers)

1. Preheat oven to 350°F. Butter a 9-inch glass or ceramic baking dish or an 8-inch square ceramic baking dish.

2. Combine everything except cherries and hollyhock petals in a blender and process until fairly smooth. Make sure you scrape down the sides of the blender so the flour doesn't sick to the sides.

3. Pour half the batter into the prepared pan. Sprinkle with cherries and half the hollyhock petals. Cover with the remaining batter. Top with the remaining hollyhock petals. Bake for about 45 minutes, or until puffed and brown; a tester inserted in the center should come out clean.

This is one of those desserts that is fantastic to slip in the oven just as you're sitting down to dinner and pull out to eat just as the main course has been cleared. Plan accordingly.

Lilacs

Botanical Name: *Syringa vulgaris*

Nicknames: Goat's rue

Language of Flowers: Purple lilacs symbolize love's first emotions, whereas white lilacs are said to indicate the innocence of youth.

Background: According to Greek mythology, Pan, the god of the forests and fields, was captivated by the beauty of a nymph named Syringa. Pan pursued Syringa with such vigor that to escape his pursuit, Syringa turned herself into an aromatic bush, which now bears her name. Lilacs bring me back to a time when I was a little girl. My grandparents had a house in the country and their yard had several large lilacs growing in it. I loved to spend time with them, and every time I smell a lilac, I think of that big old house (though perhaps it was only big in my little girl memories) and how clean and fresh everything always smelled. I would like to imagine, because my Bubbie hung the clothes out to dry, that springtime laundry smelled of lilacs, but perhaps that is just wistful thinking.

Culinary Use: Lilacs taste like they smell: fresh, heady, and sweet, with slightly bitter lemony undertones. They're most commonly used in salads, but they have many culinary applications.

Seasonality: Lilacs bloom in late spring. The flowers are not commercially available, so I suggest you grow a shrub of your own or make friends with someone who has a couple. If you live in an area with a farmers' market, it is not uncommon in spring to find a vendor who sells yard-grown unsprayed lilacs.

Preparation: Cleaning lilacs is time consuming. Halfway through cleaning a cup of lilac blossoms I have to stop and take a sniff or two to remind myself why I am doing it in the first place. Remove the flower clusters (the peduncles) from the branch. Wash the flowers and further separate the clusters. Pull each flower from its sepal (the green part at the base of the flower). You may leave the stamen and stigma at the center of each blossom intact. With all the lilacs clean, it is tempting to chuck the remainder in the compost pile, but don't; the branches of the lilac smell just as good as the blossoms when burned, so keep them around for kindling for winter's fires.

Measure: 1 cup lilacs = about 40 to 60 blossoms (from 1 stem).

Lilac Pavlova with Lime Sorbet and Lilac Blackberry Syrup

Pavlova (pronounced *pav-LOV-vuh*) is a dessert named after the Russian ballerina Anna Pavlova. Its meringue base is crisp on the outside and soft on the inside and typically crowned with whipped cream and fruit, such as strawberries, kiwi, or pomegranate seeds. Made with lilac sugar, this pavlova tastes as ethereal as it looks. I like to serve it with a little lime sorbet nestled in each lilac cloud and a drizzle of lilac blackberry syrup that lets your senses be transported. *Serves 10.*

1. Preheat oven to 210°F. Line 2 baking sheets with parchment paper.

2. Mix 4 tablespoons of the lilac sugar with cornstarch in a small bowl.

3. With a mixer on high speed, beat egg whites for 1 minute, until foamy, and then add cream of tartar. Gradually and slowly, without stopping the mixer, add the remaining sugar and beat for 4 or 5 minutes, until whites are stiff and hold their peaks. (At this point, if you wanted to, you should be able to hold the bowl upside down without the whites even threatening to fall out!)

4. Fold cornstarch mixture and lemon juice into egg whites. With an extra-large soup spoon, drop dollops of the mixture onto the prepared baking sheets. Using the back of the spoon, make an indentation in the center of each dollop and turn the spoon to widen the indentation enough to make a little bowl.

5. Bake pavlovas for about 1 hour, or until they feel dry to the touch. Turn off the oven and leave them in it for about another hour. Pavlovas don't have a long shelf life, so make them and eat them! Top each one with a scoop of lime sorbet and a few spoonfuls of lilac blackberry syrup.

MERINGUE

1 cup plus 2 tablespoons lilac sugar (page 176), divided
2 tablespoons cornstarch
4 egg whites
¼ teaspoon cream of tartar
½ teaspoon lemon juice

TOPPINGS*
1 quart lime sorbet (page 105)
About 1 cup lilac blackberry syrup (page 177)

*Or top pavlovas with whipped cream and fruit of your choice. The sky's the limit!

Foolproof Meringue

What's this about lemon juice and cornstarch? Adding cornstarch to your meringue mixture ensures that the outside of the pavlova is crisp while the inside stays soft and yielding. The lemon juice is added to help stabilize the meringue. Ideally you will make the meringue in a meticulously clean copper mixing bowl, but you can achieve a stiffer peak in any bowl by adding lemon juice.

Lime Sorbet

2 cups simple syrup (page 177)
1 cup freshly squeezed lime juice
½ teaspoon lime zest
1 cup water

Mix all ingredients in a large pitcher or liquid measuring cup. Freeze in an ice-cream maker according to manufacturer's instructions. You can keep this in the freezer for 2 or 3 months. Makes 1 quart.

My boys pour this lilac blackberry syrup on their pancakes and waffles. I like it folded into my morning yogurt with some fresh blackberries and lilac blossoms.

Lilac Sorbet

The color of this sorbet will vary depending on the color of the lilac you use. I like to use purple lilacs because the color of purple lilac sorbet is so beautiful, but white lilacs make an almost translucent confection that's perfect for a formal dinner. The flavor will vary as well, ranging from highly perfumed to subtly fragrant. *Serves 4 to 6*.

1. Place lilac blossoms in a glass bowl. Bring water, sugar, and lime juice to a boil, and then pour over flowers. Let stand for at least 10 minutes and up to 24 hours before straining out the flowers. Chill the reserved liquid for at least 2 hours.

2. Process the chilled mixture in an ice-cream maker according to manufacturer's directions. You can keep lilac sorbet in the freezer for up to 4 months for a taste of lilac long after season's end. For the best flavor, let sorbet sit at room temperature for about 15 minutes, or until it releases its chill, before serving.

2 cups lilac blossoms
2 cups water
¼ cup sugar
2 tablespoons lime juice

This is the ideal sorbet to serve in tulip cups (as on page 163), because lilacs and tulips bloom at the same time.

Oven-Baked Doughnuts with Lilac Cream Filling

Doughnuts are one of my husband's favorite treats, and there is a certain fine restaurant we go to just so he can have them for dessert. At home, I don't always want to pull out the deep fryer or put up a pot of oil, so I found a way to make delicious doughnuts in the oven. When you bite into one and taste the rich, decadent lilac cream, it is impossible to miss the frying. *Makes 12 doughnuts.*

1. Preheat oven to 350°F. Coat the wells of 12 muffin cups with nonstick spray.

2. Combine flour, cornmeal, baking powder, salt, ground cloves, and sugar in a large bowl. Make a well in the center of the dry ingredients and into it drop egg, vanilla, and oil. Stir well, but do not overmix.

3. Fill muffin cups two-thirds full with batter and bake for 25 minutes, or until a toothpick inserted in the center of a doughnut comes out with faint crumbs clinging to it.

4. To make the coating, place butter in a wide bowl. Place sugar and cardamom in a paper bag or a bowl with a lid and shake to combine. Dip each doughnut in butter and then toss in sugar mixture to coat.

5. To fill the doughnuts, spoon pastry cream into a pastry bag fitted with a plain round tip. Poke a hole in the bottom of each doughnut with the tip and squeeze about 1 tablespoon of filling in each. Eat these the same day they are made.

Lilacs finish blooming just around Mother's Day. Bake Mom a batch of lilac cream-filled doughnuts—it's better than any flower bouquet! You can also layer lilac cream with fruit and cake to make a trifle. Or mix lilac cream with a bit of fresh whipped cream to put on pancakes for a special Mother's Day breakfast in bed.

DOUGHNUTS

1¼ cups all-purpose flour

¼ cup finely ground cornmeal

2 teaspoons baking powder

¼ teaspoon salt

¼ teaspoon ground cloves

¾ cup sugar

1 egg

1 teaspoon pure vanilla extract

⅓ cup canola oil

COATING

4 tablespoons (½ stick) unsalted butter, melted

1 cup sugar

¼ teaspoon ground cardamom

FILLING

1 cup lilac pastry cream (page 183)

Coconut Lilac Tapioca

I've always loved tapioca pudding, but the first time I had it made by Claudia Fleming, it took my breath away. When I began thinking of uses for lilac, the creaminess of tapioca kept springing to mind. This dish has just enough texture from the tapioca and lilac flowers, and the coconut and lilac flavors provide a nice balance. Don't be afraid to add a spoonful of that lilac blackberry syrup (page 177) and fresh or candied lilacs on top. *Makes 6 servings.*

1. Soak tapioca in coconut milk for 1 hour, stirring occasionally to make sure you end up with individual bouncy nuggets rather than a solid lump of tapioca.

2. Combine milk and sugar in a medium saucepan over medium heat and bring to a fast simmer. Stir in tapioca with coconut milk and bring to a boil.

3. Simmer uncovered, stirring frequently, for about 1 hour, or until tapioca turns soft and translucent. Let pudding cool before stirring in lilac blossoms. Cover and refrigerate overnight or up to 1 week. Serve topped with lilac blackberry syrup and fresh or candied lilacs, if desired.

½ cup large pearl tapioca
2 (14-ounce) cans unsweetened coconut milk
3 cups whole milk
½ cup sugar
1 cup lilac blossoms
About 36 fresh and/or candied lilacs (page 176), for topping (optional)

A mix of fresh and candied flowers makes a pretty garnish.

White Pepper Thumbprint Cookies with Lilac Jam

White pepper and lilac are the stars in this cookie; both flavors are delicate, but one is spicy and the other flowery. The cookie dough is delicate, buttery, and crumbly. The flavors and textures combine for an intensely sensual experience. I dare you not to make a noise when you eat one. *Makes 18 cookies.*

1. Preheat oven to 375°F. Line 2 baking sheets with parchment paper.

2. Combine all the cookie ingredients with a mixer on medium-high speed for about 4 minutes until a shaggy, sticky dough is formed.

3. Scoop dough by the tablespoon onto prepared baking sheets, leaving 1½ inches of space around each cookie. Bake for 8 to 10 minutes, or until the edges begin to turn golden, and then make an indentation in the top of each cookie with the back of a wooden spoon. Bake for 2 minutes more, or until the edges are fully golden.

4. Place the sheets on a wire rack to cool. Drop a teaspoon of lilac jam in the center of each one. These cookies can be stored, unfilled, in an airtight container for 10 days; once filled, they should be eaten within 1 day.

WHITE PEPPER COOKIES
¼ cup confectioners' sugar
½ cup all-purpose flour
3 tablespoons cornstarch
2 tablespoons blanched almond flour
6 tablespoons cool unsalted butter
¼ teaspoon pure vanilla extract
¾ teaspoon ground white pepper

LILAC JAM FILLING
About ¾ cup lilac jam (page 180)

Flower Thumbprint Cookies
This recipe works equally well with violet, rose, or dandelion jam. You can also make other types of dough for the cookies; peanut butter is delicious filled with dandelion jam, chocolate pairs well with rose jam, and plain flower shortbread (as on page 117) works well with a myriad of jams.

Flower Jellies and Jams

See pages 179–180 to make conserves from all your favorite flavors. *From left to right:* lilac jam, apricot pineapple sage jam, violet jelly, elderflower jam, rose petal jam, and dandelion jam.

You've just got to try gourmet PB&J sandwiches with lilac or nasturtium flower jam in place of the classic grape or strawberry.

Nasturtiums

Botanical Name: *Tropaeolum*

Nicknames: Indian cress or monk's cress

Language of Flowers: Nasturtiums symbolize patriotism. (Perhaps for this reason, they were among Thomas Jefferson's favorite flowers grown at his Monticello estate.)

Background: Nasturtiums are funny plants. Extremely prolific and showy, they captured the attention and adoration of Claude Monet, who grew large swaths of them and depicted them in his work. The shape of the flower has helped name it. *Tropaeolum* comes from the Latin *tropaion*, meaning "trophy"; it refers to the shape of the helmets worn by Greek warriors. Monk's cress refers to the way the flower resembles the hood of a monk's robe. *Nasturtium* is from the Latin for "nose twist" (*nas*, meaning "nose," and *tortum*, meaning "twist"), thanks to the flower's spicy, peppery scent and the way people twist their noses when they eat it. It also happens to be the Latin name for watercress (*Nasturtium officianale*), which shares a similar flavor profile.

Culinary Use: Peppery and spicy with a bittersweet back note, nasturtium flowers and leaves are most popularly used as a salad herb. Their colors run the gamut from pale yellow to deep red and even include some pinks, so choose the color that suits you best.

Seasonality: Nasturtiums are prolific and self-seeding in summer and have a flush of blooms well into autumn. They grow easily from seed in pots on patios and in hanging baskets.

Preparation: With the exception of the seed, all parts of the nasturtium can be eaten—the flowers, leaves, and fruit. Pick the flowers from the plant, rinse them in cool water, and dry them before eating.

Measure: 1 cup nasturtiums = about 15 to 30 flowers (used whole).

Corn and Black Beans with Nasturtiums

Summer corn is sweet and juicy and has a fairly short season. I like to take advantage when it is around and put it in practically everything. Funny thing is, I feel the same way about nasturtiums, but instead of sweet and juicy, they are spicy and colorful. With black beans, this dish packs a protein punch and makes a good quick lunch, especially over a bed of fresh greens. It works equally well as a side dish for dinner. *Serves 4.*

1. Put beans in a big pot of water and boil them until they are fork-tender, about 1 hour.

   I like to cook the beans in vegetable broth seasoned with salt, pepper, a little garlic, and, if I can get my hands on it, some epazote (a pungent herb native to South America, Central America, and southern Mexico).

2. Drain beans and combine with remaining ingredients in a serving bowl. Toss, cover, and refrigerate for at least 30 minutes and up to 3 days.

1 cup black beans, soaked overnight*
Kernels from 2 ears of corn
1 red bell pepper, diced
1 red onion, diced
1 cup nasturtium flowers, roughly chopped
½ cup nasturtium leaves, roughly chopped (optional)
Juice of 1 lime
2 tablespoons extra-virgin olive oil
1 tablespoon minced cilantro
Salt and pepper to taste

*If you want to take a shortcut and use a can of black beans, please do, just make certain to rinse and drain them well.

Nasturtium Pizza

My dear friend Matt Michel caters pizza parties from his wood-oven pizza truck, Rolling in Dough. Who better to help me perfect my pizza dough than the man behind the wheel? Nasturtium petals are unexpected in pizza crust, but their peppery essence works so well. I like mine served sauceless with lots of toppings, but to each his own. *Makes two 12-inch pizzas.*

1. Put warm water, sugar, and oil in the bowl of a mixer fitted with the dough hook. Add yeast and let it sit for 10 minutes, until mixture foams. In a medium bowl, stir to combine flours, salt, and nasturtium flowers. Sprinkle flour mixture into yeast mixture. Mix on low speed for 5 minutes, until dough is smooth and bouncy. Cover the bowl with a cotton kitchen towel and let stand for about 1 hour, or until dough has doubled in volume.

2. Turn dough onto a surface dusted with flour and knead by pushing it away from your body with the heel of your hand, folding it over, and repeating about 12 times. Divide dough into two balls. At this point, dough can be baked or stored for up to 2 days in the refrigerator on a baking sheet covered with plastic wrap.

3. Preheat oven to 450°F. Rub two baking sheets with olive oil and dust with semolina flour. Stretch out each dough ball by tapping and pressing outward from the center with your fingertips. Transfer to prepared baking sheets. Cover with toppings of your choice. Bake pizzas for 20 to 25 minutes, rotating sheets halfway through baking so the dough browns evenly. Slice, serve, and enjoy.

NASTURTIUM FLOWER DOUGH

1 cup warm water

1 teaspoon sugar

2 tablespoons extra-virgin olive oil, plus more for pan

1 (¼-ounce) packet active dried yeast (about 1¼ teaspoons)

2½ cups high-gluten bread flour

1 cup semolina flour,* plus more for dusting

1½ teaspoons salt

1 cup nasturtium flowers

*If you can't find semolina, substitute high-gluten bread flour.

TOPPINGS

About 3 tablespoons extra-virgin olive oil

⅓ cup herb flower pesto (page 72)

About ½ cup (4 ounces) goat cheese

⅓ cup nasturtium flowers

Other toppings of your choice

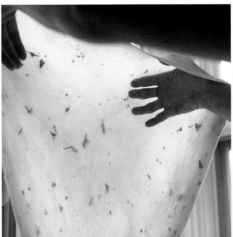
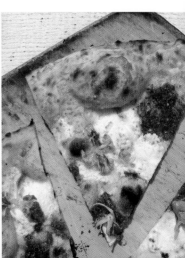

Goat Cheese Nasturtium Ice Cream

I can't resist goat cheese. Hard, soft, aged, fresh—I love it all. With the addition of nasturtiums, this goat cheese ice cream treads the line between sweet and savory (like most of my favorite indulgences). In fact, if you want to push it up to the top of your menu, you could serve it with savory toppings such as caramelized onions, crunchy bacon pieces, or spiced nuts and call it an appetizer. Try it; see if anyone argues. *Makes about 2 quarts.*

1. Put goat cheese in a large (3-quart) heatproof container that has a lid.

2. In a medium saucepan over medium heat, warm milk and stir in half the sugar. Simmer until sugar dissolves. Meanwhile, whisk yolks with the remaining sugar and salt in a heatproof bowl. When the milk has absorbed all the sugar—but before it comes to a boil—begin to temper your eggs by slowly pouring half the warm milk mixture over the yolk mixture while whisking vigorously. Then slowly pour the egg-milk mixture back into the saucepan, whisking vigorously. Heat mixture until it coats the back of a spoon and the temperature reaches 165°F on a candy thermometer.

3. Slowly pour mixture over goat cheese, whisking to fully dissolve and incorporate it. Fold in chopped flowers and chill mixture for at least 4 hours and up to overnight. Freeze in an ice-cream maker according to manufacturer's instructions. Let ice cream sit at room temperature for about 15 minutes before serving.

1 cup (8 ounces) goat cheese*
1½ cups milk
⅔ cup sugar, divided
6 egg yolks
Pinch sea salt
⅓ cup nasturtium flowers, finely
   chopped

*Fresh, soft goat cheese is ideal for making ice cream.

The flowers will release their essential oils when they absorb some of the residual heat from the cream.

Nasturtium Thumbprint Cookies

With their pretty orange centers and dough studded with petals, these cookies look like a spot of sunshine on a plate. Their sunny expressiveness belies their complex and slightly spicy taste. *Makes about 48 cookies.*

1. Line 2 baking sheets with parchment paper.

2. Beat butter, sugars, and vanilla with a mixer on medium-high speed for 3 minutes, or until creamy. Lower mixer speed and beat in flour, white pepper, salt, and nasturtium flowers, mixing just until evenly distributed.

   Don't mix this dough too much; the crumb on these cookies should be delicate.

3. Scoop dough into 1-inch balls, or pat dough to about ¾-inch thick and cut out cookies with a 1-inch blossom-shaped cookie cutter. Place cookies about 1 inch apart on the prepared baking sheets, pressing indentations into the centers with a finger. Freeze sheets for about 1 hour.

   Resting the dough provides a little insurance that cookies will not spread when they are baking. I bake mine straight from the freezer.

4. Preheat oven to 325°F. Fill cookies with nasturtium jam and bake for 18 to 20 minutes, or until the edges start to turn golden and the bottoms are brown. Let cool on a wire rack before eating. Store these cookies between layers of parchment in a tin for up to about 1 week.

1 cup (2 sticks) unsalted butter, room temperature
⅓ cup sugar
1 tablespoon confectioners' sugar
½ teaspoon pure vanilla extract
2 cups all-purpose flour
½ teaspoon ground white pepper
½ teaspoon salt
½ cup nasturtium flowers, finely chopped
½ cup nasturtium jam (page 180)*

*Nasturtium cookie dough also pairs well with dandelion, pineapple sage, or violet jams.

Orchids

Botanical Name: *Vanilla*, *Dendrobium*, and *Cymbidium* are the edible species of orchids.

Nicknames: Snake orchid, bridal veil orchid, spring orchid

Language of Flowers: Orchids signify refinement, as well as the innocence of children.

Background: The word *orchid* comes from the Greek *orchis*, which means "testicle," because the roots closely resemble that part of the male anatomy. According to Greek mythology, Orchis was the son of a nymph and a satyr. He made a terrible scene at a Bacchanalian party, drinking and carousing and assaulting a priestess. So the Bacchanalians destroyed Orchis. But at his father's urging, the gods took pity and turned him into a flower.

Culinary Use: The petals taste of cucumber and endive and are popularly used in stir-fries, dessert decorations, and a Turkish ice cream called *sahlep*.

Seasonality: Seasonal availability varies. Year-round, you can purchase orchids for eating either online (see "Sources," page 186) or at an organic produce shop or Asian market. As with any edible flower, be sure to avoid florists' flowers, which have likely been sprayed with chemicals.

Preparation: Orchid flowers can be eaten after you've removed them from their stems, given them a quick rinse, and dried them well.

Measure: 1 cup orchids = petals from 10 to 15 large orchids, or about 50 small orchids (used whole).

Thai Orchid and Beef Salad

With a friend by your side, work and play are often indistinguishable. I am lucky to work with a dear friend who is also incredibly talented and versatile; she has an amazing palate in addition to an ability to make me laugh heartily and often. I asked Nanao to contribute her recipe for this salad, knowing she would have a quick and easy way to make something beautiful and complex. As always, she is right on the mark! *Serves 4.*

1. Grill steak to medium-rare and let it rest 10 minutes before slicing it thinly across the grain.

2. In a serving bowl, toss sliced steak with red onion, cilantro, and orchids.

3. Whisk fish sauce, lime juice, sugar, and chili flakes until sugar dissolves. Pour sauce over salad, add scallions, and toss. This dish keeps overnight and serves well hot or cold.

1 pound flank steak
½ cup thinly sliced red onion
Handful fresh cilantro
About 24 small or 8 large orchid
   flowers (about 1 cup)
3 tablespoons fish sauce
3 tablespoons fresh lime juice
2 teaspoons sugar
2 teaspoons red chili flakes
2 scallions, thinly sliced

Orchid Seafood Sauté

Lucky am I to live in a place where we get to eat fresh fish most of the year. In high summer, it is nice to have an easy dinner of seafood sauté and complement it with the bright, fresh crunch of orchid. *Serves 4.*

1. Soak rice noodles in warm water for about 1 hour, until tender. Drain.

2. Put 1 tablespoon each of the oil and butter in a large skillet over medium heat. Cook and stir onion and bell pepper until onion is translucent and just barely starting to soften, about 5 minutes. Add snow peas and cook and stir for about 2 minutes more. Remove skillet from heat and transfer vegetables to a serving dish.

3. Put skillet back on the stove and add the remaining oil and butter. Add monkfish and cook and stir for about 1 minute, then add shrimp. Cook for 1 minute more and then stir in scallops. Cook and stir mixture for a few minutes more, or until fish is opaque. Remove skillet from heat and transfer fish mixture to the serving dish with the vegetables.

4. Return skillet to heat and make the sauce by bringing all the remaining ingredients except cornstarch and orchids to a boil. In a bowl, mix cornstarch with ½ cup water to form a slurry and stir it into the boiling sauce. Cook and stir sauce for about 5 minutes, or until it reaches the thickness you like.

5. Transfer everything from the serving dish back to the skillet with the sauce. Cook and stir it all together for just less than 1 minute. Put drained rice noodles in the serving bowl, add vegetables and fish coated in sauce, top with orchids, and serve.

1 (8-ounce) package rice noodles
2 tablespoons extra-virgin olive oil, divided
2 tablespoons unsalted butter, divided
1 red onion, cut in half moons
1 red bell pepper, cut in half moons
½ cup snow peas, thinly sliced
½ pound monkfish fillet, cubed
½ pound shrimp, peeled and deveined
¼ pound scallops
1 cup pineapple chunks
½ teaspoon red pepper flakes
½ teaspoon salt
½ teaspoon freshly minced ginger
2 tablespoons packed brown sugar
2 tablespoons rice wine vinegar
2 tablespoons tamari*
1 teaspoon cornstarch
8 orchid flowers

*Like soy sauce, tamari is made from fermented soybeans. But it's richer, darker, and less salty, with more of a smooth, mellow flavor. In a pinch, substitute tamari with an equal amount of soy sauce.

Clockwise, from above: Thai Orchid and Beef Salad (page 120), Hibiscus Fried Rice (page 92), Stuffed Squash Blossoms (page 150), and Orchid Seafood Sauté (page 121).

Mango Orchid Sticky Rice

Sticky rice is popular in both sweet and savory Asian dishes. Here's a twist on the classic dessert sticky rice, bursting with coconut mango flavor and crisp little orchids. *Serves 4.*

1. Soak rice overnight in enough water to cover it by at least 2 inches. You could take a shortcut by several hours, but you must soak the rice regardless, so you may as well soak overnight.

   The cooking of this rice is pretty flexible if you don't have a traditional Thai rice steamer. They are pretty cool though, so check one out if you have the chance.

2. Drain rice. Line a steamer or colander with cheesecloth and pour rice into cheesecloth. Put a few inches of water and coconut water in a pot large enough to hold the steamer, drop it in, and cover with a lid (or an inverted heatproof bowl). Over medium heat, simmer coconut water for 20 to 25 minutes; halfway through the cooking time, stir rice from the bottom to the top of the steamer so that it steams evenly. When rice is done steaming, it will be translucent and still have a little bit of bite. Turn off the heat and keep rice covered for 5 to 10 more minutes.

3. In a small saucepan over medium-low heat, warm coconut milk, sugar, and salt until sugar dissolves.

4. Divide mango slices evenly among 4 plates. Arrange mounds of rice on top of the mango slices. Tuck 2 orchids into each mound of rice, and pour some of the warm coconut sauce over top.

1 cup Thai sticky rice*
1 (14-ounce) bottle coconut water
1 (14-ounce) can or bottle coconut milk
4 tablespoons sugar
Pinch salt
1 to 2 mangoes, peeled and sliced
8 orchids

*I love making this dish with black sticky rice because the color is fabulous, but you can use white if that is what you can find. If you have both, feel free to mix them; the result will be slightly purple.

Orchid Pineapple Upside-Down Cake

Pineapple upside-down cake was first made in the 1920s by a clever baker entering a canned pineapple contest. I think this interpretation deserves a small prize for using fresh pineapple and orchids instead of canned pineapple and maraschino cherries, and my son Jordan agrees. *Makes one 9- or 10-inch cake.*

1. Preheat oven to 350°F. Coat the bottom and sides of a 9- or 10-inch round cake pan with 1 tablespoon of the butter.

2. Melt the remaining 4 tablespoons of butter in a saucepan over medium heat. Add brown sugar and cook and stir for 3 to 4 minutes, until mixture is foamy and pale. Pour it into the prepared pan. Arrange pineapple rings and orchids in the bottom of the pan. I like to make sure the orchids are perfectly centered in the rings, with their wings spread and covered with caramel.

3. Whisk flour, cornmeal, baking powder, and salt together in a small bowl.

4. Beat butter and all but 2 tablespoons of the sugar with a mixer on high speed for 2 to 3 minutes, until light and fluffy. Add egg yolks and vanilla and beat for 5 minutes more on high speed, until mixture is smooth and pale yellow. Gradually beat in dry ingredients on low speed. Your mixture is going to be a little stiff, but that's OK.

5. In a clean, dry bowl, beat egg whites with a mixer fitted with the whisk attachment for about 1 minute, or until they are soft and foamy. Add the remaining 2 tablespoons sugar. Continue beating whites for 5 to 8 minutes more, until they have tripled in volume and hold nice stiff peaks.

6. Gently fold about a third of the whites into the batter to lighten mixure and then add the remainder of the whites. Gently pour batter over caramel–pineapple mixture and orchids in pan.

7. Bake for about 45 minutes to an hour, until a tester inserted into the cake (but not the pineapple or caramel) comes out clean. Let cake rest for 3 to 5 minutes before inverting onto a serving plate. This beauty stays good for about 5 days at room temperature if wrapped tightly.

CARAMEL PINEAPPLE MIXTURE

5 tablespoons unsalted butter, room temperature, divided
¾ cup packed dark brown sugar
1 small pineapple, peeled, cored, and cut into rings
5 orchid flowers

PINEAPPLE CAKE

1½ cups all-purpose flour
3 tablespoons coarsely ground cornmeal
1½ teaspoons baking powder
½ teaspoon salt
½ cup (1 stick) unsalted butter, room temperature
1 cup sugar, divided
4 eggs, separated
1½ teaspoons pure vanilla extract
⅓ cup pineapple juice or milk

Passionfruit Orchid Tartlets

One of our favorite flavor combinations at Mali B is coconut and passionfruit. How can you go wrong? We always add a third flavor for balance—sometimes blackberry, sometimes rosemary. Here, a coconut cookie crust sits pretty with passionfruit curd and orchids atop. The flowers add their crisp texture and cool, slightly bitter taste to round out the flavor profile, not to mention looking gorgeous on top of the finished tarts. *Makes eight 3-inch tarts or twelve 2-inch tarts.*

1. Preheat oven to 300°F. Thoroughly coat the insides of your tartlet pans with cooking spray.

2. Spread coconut on a baking sheet and toast it—tossing occasionally, for a consistent golden brown—in the oven for about 15 minutes, or until the flakes are mostly golden brown.

3. In the bowl of a food processor, process coconut with egg white until finely ground and completely mixed. Press mixture into the bottoms and up the sides of the tart shells. Bake the shells just until they start to turn golden brown, 12 to 15 minutes.

4. To make the curd, mix yolks and sugar together in a medium saucepan. When they are fully mixed, add passionfruit puree, butter, and salt. Put pan over medium heat and stir for about 15 minutes, until mixture thickens and begins to bubble. I am a fan of multitasking, but not this time—don't walk away while the curd cooks.

5. You can immediately spoon passionfruit curd into the tart shells or you can put it in a container, cover with plastic wrap, and refrigerate for up to 2 weeks. Top the tarts with candied orchids and serve.

3 cups sweetened coconut flakes
1 egg white
4 egg yolks
½ cup sugar
½ cup passionfruit puree
4 tablespoons (½ stick) unsalted butter
Pinch salt
36 micro orchids* or 8 to 12 large orchids, fresh and/or candied (page 176)

*Micro orchids are just what they sound like: mini orchids. To try them, see "Sources," page 186.

Orchids of all sizes are particularly easy to candy. Both fresh and candied orchids look and taste fantastic in these tartlets.

Pansies and Violas

Botanical Name: *Viola* (both pansies and violas)

Nicknames: Call me to you, pink-eyed-John, love true (pansies); Johnny-jump-ups (violas)

Language of Flowers: Both pansies and violas signify loving thoughts.

Background: Pansy's name comes from the French *pensée* meaning "thought," because the flower resembles a face deep in thought.

Pansies appear in German legend as once having had a sweet scent that would draw people in to smell from miles away; the grass that served as feed for cattle became trampled, so the pansy prayed to God for help and was granted great beauty but no scent.

Another interesting Arthurian tale features pansies as fortunetellers. It was said that a knight would look to a pansy petal for a glimpse into his future. Thick left-leaning lines foretold a life of trouble, whereas right-leaning lines predicted prosperity and good fortune. The number of lines told of luck in love (or lack thereof).

Culinary Uses: Pansies and violas have a mild, slightly lemony taste with a wintergreen note. They are popularly used in salads and as decoration on soft cheeses.

Seasonality: Pansies and violas are the lovely unassuming heralds of spring. One of the first flowers to make an appearance in flowerpots and beds, pansies and violas beckon us with their facelike features. Blooming in spring throughout summer and into fall, pansies can be purchased at garden centers, nurseries, and even supermarkets; they can be grown in pots or in the ground.

Preparation: Separate each pansy or viola flower from its sepal (green base), then wash and pat dry.

Measure: 1 cup pansies = about 50 to 70 flowers (used whole).

Pansy Petal Pancakes

Spring, summer, and fall, pansies decorate my pancake plates. These pancakes are really crepes, so the batter can be made the night before—give it a gentle shake in the morning, and it's ready to go. It's fun to see a little flower peeking up at you from the plate. Served with a floral syrup, it is a great way to wake up in the morning. *Makes 12 crepes.*

1. Place all ingredients except pansy flowers in a blender. Blend until smooth. Refrigerate at least 2 hours and up to overnight.

2. Let batter come to room temperature before frying. Shake well. Heat a non-stick skillet over medium heat until a bit of butter melts quickly when added to it.

3. Lift skillet from heat and pour ¼ cup of the batter in the middle, tilting and swirling the pan to distribute it quickly and evenly. Return to heat. After about 1 minute, sprinkle with pansies. Use a spatula to loosen the edges of the crepe from the sides of the skillet. Flip crepe and cook for another 30 seconds. Turn or slide it onto a serving plate. Repeat with remaining batter.

These get easier to make as you go. Consider the first crepe a sacrificial one—not so pretty, but tasty enough for the cook!

1½ cups milk
½ cup water
1 tablespoon sugar
¼ teaspoon salt
3 tablespoons unsalted butter, melted,* plus more for cooking
½ cup buckwheat flour
¾ cup all-purpose flour
3 eggs
12 pansy flowers (about 1 cup)
Pansy simple syrup or flower syrup of any kind (page 177), for topping if desired

*You can substitute vegetable oil, if you like.

You won't believe the color of syrup made with dark purple or black pansies. The resulting liquid is a blueish hue so beautiful and unusual, you'll have a hard time convincing friends that you didn't use food coloring to achieve it.

Pansy Lollipops

Every time we make these at Mali B, they elicit *oohs* and *ahhs* from our clients and customers. I like to make them free-form (without a candy mold), but you can use hard-candy molds if you prefer perfectly formed pops. This is one of those recipes where you have to decide whether to use organic sugar. We do, but it gives our pops a less-than-clear look. So if it's clarity you want, go for refined sugar. A silicone baking mat (such as Silpat) is a necessity if you don't use hard-candy molds. *Makes 10 lollipops.*

Lollipop sticks
12 to 18 (about 1 cup) viola flowers*
1 cup sugar
½ cup corn syrup
⅓ cup water

*You can substitute Johnny-jump-ups or pansies or violets if you prefer. These flowers work well in lollipops because they flatten nicely.

1. If you're using a mold, coat it with nonstick spray and insert pop sticks in the cavities. If you're making free-form pops, line a baking sheet or a piece of marble with a silicone baking mat. Place lollipop sticks about 3 inches apart. Put 1 viola flower in each mold or at the base of each lollipop stick on the baking mat.

2. Place a large metal bowl full of ice cubes next to the cooking surface. Combine sugar, corn syrup, and water in a saucepan over medium heat and stir until sugar is dissolved. Then let it come to a boil and insert a candy thermometer. Boil syrup mixture without stirring until the temperature reaches 305°F. Remove from heat and immediately place the saucepan on top of the ice to stop the cooking.

3. Carefully pour hot syrup into candy molds or drizzle it over flowers. Let pops cool completely, about 20 minutes, before moving.

   Pansy petal pops are best stored standing up. Use a piece of styrofoam or poke holes in the lid of a plastic food container to keep pops upright and separated. Keep away from humidity.

Pansy Tea Sandwiches

Traditional afternoon tea is a meal that has fallen out of fashion, but I think it has its place. Tea sandwiches are perfect when you want something light and delicate livened up with flowers. Serve these for a birthday or Mother's Day luncheon or put them on your Easter plate. *Makes 24 sandwiches.*

1. Slice cucumber as thinly as possible, using a mandoline if you have one. Lay slices on a paper towel to absorb excess moisture.

2. Stir to thoroughly combine cream cheese and goat cheese in a small bowl. Gently stir pansy flowers into cheese mixture.

3. Spread a thin layer of cheese mixture onto each slice of bread. Arrange a single layer of cucumber slices on half of the bread slices. Place remaining bread slices on top, cheese side down.

4. Trim crusts. Slice sandwiches in quarters diagonally so each sandwich makes 4 triangles.

Nasturtium Tea Sandwiches
Use goat cheese, nasturtium flowers and chopped leaves, and butter on whole wheat bread.

Pineapple Sage and Ham Tea Sandwiches
Use pineapple sage flowers and finely chopped pineapple sage leaves, thinly sliced ham, and a thin layer of butter and Dijon mayonnaise on rye bread.

For a pretty touch, spread the edges of the sandwiches with a thin layer of butter, and then dip the buttered edges in roughly chopped petals.

1 seedless cucumber

1 (8-ounce) package cream cheese, room temperature

4 ounces goat cheese, room temperature

24 pansy flowers, sliced chiffonade-style

12 very thin slices white bread

How to Chiffonade
Chiffonade might sound fancy—the term is French—but it's really a simple method of cutting things in long, thin strips. Stack petals or leaves and then roll them in a tight cigarlike roll. Cut across the roll with a sharp knife. This technique is a time-saver that minimizes bruising that can happen when cutting flower petals and herbs.

Serve a variety of flower tea sandwiches together with a refreshing flower spritzer and some flower petal shortbread, and you've got yourself a party.

Pansy Rhubarb Galettes

Pansies begin to show their blooms about the same time rhubarb stalks are ready to harvest, so I love to mix the two in these rustic open-face tarts. You could make one large galette rather than ten small ones, but this way everyone gets more crust. And frankly this is one dessert I don't like to share. *Makes 8 small galettes.*

1. Preheat oven to 400°F. Line two baking sheets with parchment paper.

2. In a large nonreactive bowl, toss together rhubarb, sugar, cornstarch, salt, nutmeg, and half the pansy petals.

3. Roll out dough rounds until they are thin and about 6 inches in diameter. Place them on baking sheets about 2 inches apart.

4. Heap about a half cup of the rhubarb mixture into the center of each round. Gather dough around filling, pinching the edges but leaving the center open.

5. Bake galettes for 30 minutes, or until the crust is a deep golden brown and the filling is oozy and soft. Sprinkle the remaining pansy petals over top. Serve warm, drizzled with pansy syrup, if desired.

Because the season for pansies is long, you can make this recipe well into fall by substituting other fruits for the rhubarb, such as peaches, apricots, figs, or berries.

6 cups rhubarb (about 2 pounds), cut into ½-inch pieces
1 cup pansy sugar (page 176)
2 tablespoons cornstarch
¼ teaspoon sea salt
⅛ teaspoon nutmeg
½ cup pansy or viola petals
2 standard pie crusts (store-bought or homemade),* divided into 8 rounds

Pansy simple syrup (page 177), for serving (optional)

*You can use the pie crust recipe on page 96; just omit hibiscus petals and double the recipe.

Roses

Botanical Name: *Rosa*

Nicknames: None known. (Though in *Romeo and Juliet* Shakespeare wrote that "a rose by any other name would smell as sweet.")

Language of Flowers: Every color of rose has a different meaning: White is unacquainted love, girlhood, or chastity; peach is modesty; coral is desire or passion; orange is fascination; yellow is infidelity (or joy and friendship, according to some sources); pale pink is joy or grace; pink is desire, passion, or joy of life; dark pink is gratitude; red is passionate love; red and white together are unity; burgundy is unconscious beauty; purple is enchantment; and lavender (pale purple) is love at first sight.

Background: According to Greek mythology, Aphrodite made the rose from a combination of her tears and the blood of her lover Adonis. Roman lore, on the other hand, says that the rose was created when the Gods came together at the behest of Flora, goddess of spring, to memorialize one of her nymphs. Flora gathered a bowl of petals to which each god presented a different gift; one god granted life, another lent nectar, one contributed thorns, and yet another lent fragrance.

An ancient Hindu writing tells of an argument between Vishnu and Brahma over the most beautiful flower. Brahma was ultimately swayed to believe that the rose was the most beautiful, and Vishnu's wife, Lakshmi, was created from rose petals as a reward for Vishnu's loyalty.

Culinary Use: Roses are sweet and highly aromatic. Color does not affect the flavor of roses, but scent does. The stronger the scent of the rose, the stronger the taste. And if it smells good, chances are it will taste good.

Seasonality: Roses generally bloom in early summer. Some are ever-blooming and continue to produce blossoms throughout the summer and autumn. Others have two flushes, one in early summer and again in high summer.

Preparation: Roses are a favorite hiding place of earwigs, those prehistoric-looking monster bugs with a front pincher. To make sure you don't eat any, wash your roses well. Immerse them in water and swish them around. Gently pull the petals apart from the center and cut off any white at the base, because it is bitter.

Measure: 1 cup rose petals = petals from 4 flowers up to about 16 flowers, depending on the rose.

Cardamom Cake with Raspberry Rose Mascarpone

When customers at our shop ask what cardamom is, we always say it is an Indian spice that is spicy, sweet, and pungent all at the same time. I always held to that line until my brother-in-law Ed informed me that cardamom is used liberally in Finnish cuisine. So I suppose this lovely spice has earned its place in culinary traditions around the world. But whatever food cardamom is used in, it is delicious. In this stunning cake, the warmth of cardamom complements the heady sweetness of smooth raspberry rose mascarpone and fresh tart berries. *Makes one 8-inch three-layer cake.*

1. Preheat oven to 350°F. Coat three 8-inch pans with nonstick spray and line the bottoms with parchment. Pour 2/3 cup of the milk into a liquid measuring cup and add egg whites and vanilla. Set aside.

2. With a mixer on low speed, combine cake flour, sugar, baking powder, salt, and cardamom. Add the remaining 1 cup milk and mix for about 30 seconds on low speed, until flour is moistened. Add butter. Turn mixer to medium-high speed and let it run for 2 minutes, until no lumps of butter remain.

3. Whisk to combine the egg white–vanilla mixture. Add it to the batter one-third at a time, beating for 2 minutes after each addition. Divide batter among the prepared pans. Bake for about 25 minutes, until cake pulls away from the edges and a tester inserted in the center comes out clean.

4. Cool cake layers in their pans for 15 minutes before turning them out onto a wire rack. Wait another hour or so until they're completely cool before assembling the cake.

5. For the frosting, drop rose petals into heavy cream. Cover and refrigerate for at least 2 hours and up to overnight. Strain cream directly into the bowl of a mixer fitted with a whisk attachment. Add mascarpone, confectioners' sugar, and rose syrup. Whip on high speed and watch mixer as cream changes

CAKE

1⅔ cups milk, divided

8 egg whites

3¾ teaspoons pure vanilla extract

2¼ cups sifted cake flour

2½ cups sugar

6⅔ teaspoons baking powder

1¼ teaspoons salt

1 tablespoon cardamom

1½ cups (3 sticks) butter, room temperature

RASPBERRY ROSE MASCARPONE

⅓ cup rose petals (from about 3 medium roses)

1 cup heavy cream

2 cups (1 pound) mascarpone cheese

4 tablespoons confectioners' sugar

1 tablespoons rose simple syrup (page 177)

2½ cups fresh raspberries

Candied rose petals (page 176) for topping (optional)

Mixed berries for topping (optional)

from thick to watery and back to thick again, about 4 minutes in all. Mix in raspberries.

I like to have my raspberries blended in and broken up but with visible chunks.

6. Level cakes, cutting off any dome that might have formed using a serrated knife and a gentle sawing motion. Place one layer on a serving plate. Slather the top with one-third of the mascarpone and top with the second cake layer. Cover with another third of the mascarpone. Place the final layer on top and use the remaining mascarpone to finish the cake. I like to serve this cake as is, but it really does look pretty with candied (or fresh) rose petals and some fresh berries on top.

Plan ahead: This cake doesn't store well for long once it's frosted. So, if you need to, bake the cake layers the day before you want to serve them and cover each layer tightly in plastic wrap.

raspberries
mascarpone
heavy cream
cardamom
roses
sugar
butter

Pistachio Rose Shortbread

You could argue that this shortbread is a health food. How can something with this much butter be called healthy, you ask? Pistachios are chock-full of nutrients. They contain fatty acids, antioxidants, carotenes, vitamin E, B-complex vitamins, and minerals, not to mention protein. And then there are roses, which lend flavonoids, quercetin, and vitamin C. So you see, an argument for a health cookie could be made . . . *Makes one 9-inch square pan.*

1. Preheat oven to 350°F. Line a 9-inch square pan with foil and place a square of parchment on the bottom of the pan.

   Lining the pan with foil and parchment makes it easy to remove the short-bread from the pan while it's still hot.

2. Sift flours and salt together three times.

3. With a mixer on medium-high speed, cream butter for 2 minutes or until smooth. Slowly beat in sugar until it is fully integrated. Mix in half the flour. Add pistachios, rose water, and rose petals. Turn mixer to low speed and beat in the remaining flour, being careful not to overmix.

4. Press dough into the prepared pan, again very gently. Bake for about 50 minutes, until lightly golden brown on top. Remove shortbread from the pan and cut it into 1½-inch squares. Spread shortbread squares on a baking sheet and bake them for about 5 minutes more, until the edges are a little golden. This shortbread can be stored for up to 10 days in a tin or a foil-lined container.

Flower Petal Shortbread
Skip the pistachios. Add 1½ teaspoons pure vanilla extract in place of the rose water and ¾ cup flower petals (assorted, or all of one kind) in place of the roses.

1¾ cups all-purpose flour
½ cup rice flour*
¼ teaspoon salt
1 cup (2 sticks) unsalted butter, room temperature
½ cup sugar
2 tablespoons finely ground pistachios
1 tablespoon rose water
¼ cup rose petals

*Rice flour is made from rice and contains no gluten. It makes baked goods like shortbread light and crumbly. Find it at Asian supermarkets or online, or substitute all-purpose flour in a pinch.

Flower Cookies
Try these flower cookies and more. *Clockwise from left:* pistachio rose shortbread, dianthus spiced chocolate cookies, lavender cookies, chocolate-dipped orange geranium cookies, nasturtium thumbprint cookies, sweet William shortbread, herb flower shortbread, and calendula cookies.

Fig and Rose Cream Trifle

Between the juicy figs, rich cream, and fragrant roses, this dessert is practically oozing with sensuality. I don't need to say more—try it at least once. *Serves 8.*

1. Preheat oven to 350°F. Coat a 9-inch square pan with nonstick spray and line the bottom with parchment paper.

2. Melt butter and saffron together in a saucepan over low heat or in the microwave. Stir in milk.

3. In the bowl of a mixer fitted with the whisk attachment, beat eggs and sugar on medium-high speed for about 5 minutes, until they are opaque.

   If using organic sugar, there will be some visible granules in the beaten eggs at this point. The eggs will likely be smooth if you use granulated sugar.

4. Add flour, baking powder, and salt to egg mixture and mix briefly. When no streaks of flour remain, pour in the saffron-infused butter and milk mixture. Mix gently with the mixer or by hand until all the liquid is incorporated. Pour batter into the prepared pan and bake for 40 to 45 minutes, or until a tester inserted into the center comes out clean. Let cool for at least 30 minutes and up to overnight.

5. Cut figs into quarters. Cut cake into 1-by-2-inch rectangles. Grab a shallow bowl and place some cake cubes in the bottom. Top that with some rose cream and then figs. Keep layering cake, cream, and figs until you run out of ingredients. I like to end with a bit of cream and top the trifle with rose petals. It will last for 3 days as is; the cream will lose its cohesiveness, but it will absorb into the cake so nicely.

1 cup (2 sticks) unsalted butter, room temperature
½ teaspoon saffron
¾ cup milk, room temperature
2 eggs
1½ cups sugar
1¾ cups all-purpose flour
2 teaspoons baking powder
¼ teaspoon salt
¼ teaspoon pure vanilla extract
2 pints fresh, juicy figs
3 cups rose petal whipped cream (page 183)
Rose petals, for topping (optional)

Squash Blossoms

Botanical Name: *Cucurbita*

Nicknames: Kalabasa

Language of Flowers: There are no references to squash blossoms in the Victorian language of flowers.

Background: Squash is one of the "three sisters," the three crops frequently grown together by Native Americans because they complement one another. The stalk of corn provided support for beans and shade for squash, and all three together provided a healthy diet.

Culinary Use: Delicate, sweet, and vegetal, squash blossoms are most commonly stuffed with goat cheese or other fillings and sometimes fried. I imagined squash blossoms would have a more coarse, dry texture and almost no taste, but instead I was pleasantly surprised to feel the deliciousness of the blossom. It took no time at all for me to decide I would rather have the blossom than the squash.

Seasonality: Flowering in late spring through late summer, squash buds and blossoms are easy to grow or buy at your local farmers' market.

Preparation: Like all edible flowers, squash blossoms should be washed and dried before eating. Store-bought squash blossoms generally already have the pistils removed, but if yours do not, make sure you reach inside the blossom and gently tug at the pistil and pull it out.

Measure: 1 cup squash blossoms = about 3 to 6 blossoms (used whole).

Squash Blossom Tempura

Lovely squash blossom, the belle of the ball, I'm going to fry you! I know a score of people who think anything tastes better fried. (You know who you are, Andrew Fischel, and your deep-fried Oreos!) I try to stay away from fried foods, but offer me a little tempura and I'm beyond tempted. Squash blossom tempura rocks the house. *Serves 4.*

Grapeseed oil or other clean-frying vegetable oil*
1 cup ice-cold seltzer water
¾ cup all-purpose flour
¼ cup cornstarch
12 squash blossoms
Salt and pepper to taste

*How much oil you need will depend on the size of the pot you use.

1. Fill a large heavy-bottom pot with at least 4 or 5 inches of oil. Warm oil to almost 400°F.

2. In a deep bowl, whisk seltzer, flour, and cornstarch to form a slurry with the consistency of thick cream. Dip blossoms in batter one at a time, coating them and gently shaking off excess.

3. Fry small batches of coated flowers for about 2 minutes each, until they are golden brown. Drain on paper towels, if necessary, and season with salt and pepper while still hot.

Don't stop with squash blossoms; tempura flowers of all kinds are remarkable. Try dianthus, calendula, hibiscus, elderflower, and nasturtium.

Baby Squash with Squash Blossoms

This summer side dish is a delectable way for you to make use of summer squash when it is still in baby form and before it gets so large that you have to beg friends to take it off your hands or try *another* version of your chocolate zucchini muffins or zucchini bread. Sounds like I've been there? Yes, I speak from experience when I tell you that, when you serve this dish, your neighbors will no longer pretend not to know you throughout squash season. *Serves 6.*

1 tablespoon herb butter or herb flower butter (page 178)
1 quart baby summer squash
12 to 15 squash blossoms, halved lengthwise and quartered
½ teaspoon sea salt, plus more to taste
Freshly ground pepper to taste
2 tablespoons good Parmigiano-Reggiano cheese, finely grated

1. Melt herb butter in a nonstick skillet over medium heat. Toss in squash and cook, stirring frequently, until squash releases its juices and begins to caramelize. Turn cooked squash into a serving dish and cover.

2. Add squash blossoms to the hot skillet. Let the residual heat from the skillet warm them for about 30 seconds, until they are just beginning to wilt. Add them to the dish, season with salt, pepper, and cheese, and serve warm.

Squash Blossom Quesadillas

Busy days call for quick and easy dinners, and these quesadillas fit the bill. They have a little protein, a little vegetable, and a little carbohydrate; plus, they reheat well, so I can make a bunch of extras and have enough for the next day's lunch. *Makes 6 quesadillas.*

1. Warm oil in a nonstick skillet over medium heat. Add onion and cook until it softens and begins to turn translucent. Add squash blossoms and salt, cooking and stirring until blossoms wilt and liquid in pan evaporates. Stir in roasted pepper and remove from heat.

2. Melt just a bit of butter in a cast-iron pan or griddle over medium-low heat. Place a tortilla on the skillet and heat it until it puffs slightly, flip it, and arrange a few spoonfuls of squash-blossom filling on top. Sprinkle with about ¼ cup of the queso fresco and top with another tortilla. Wait about 2 minutes—depending on how hot your pan is—until cheese has melted and tortillas have more or less fused together, and then flip quesadilla and cook on the other side for about 1 minute more. Repeat with the rest of the quesadillas. Serve warm.

Portable Quesadillas
Wrap cooled quesadillas individually in foil, pop them in the refrigerator, and then reheat them one at a time in the pan, still wrapped in the foil, for a quick snack.

SQUASH BLOSSOM FILLING
1 tablespoon extra-virgin olive oil
1 small onion, diced
About 24 squash blossoms, stemmed and roughly chopped
Salt, to taste
1 poblano or red bell pepper, roasted* and diced

2 tablespoons (¼ stick) unsalted butter, divided
12 corn tortillas
1½ cups grated queso fresco,** divided

*With tongs, rotate pepper over an open flame. When the skin begins to blacken, put it in a paper bag and seal it. Let it sit for about 5 minutes and then remove it, remove the stem, and peel it. The blackened skin will come right off.

**Queso fresco is a fresh white Mexican cheese that melts beautifully.

Stuffed Squash Blossoms

Most stuffed squash blossoms call for a heaping helping of cheese, a dip in batter, and a bath in hot oil. For something a little lighter, I stuff squash blossoms with one of my favorite grains, quinoa. I call for goat cheese, but you may choose to skip that ingredient if you prefer. *Serves 3 to 4.*

1. Warm oil in a medium skillet over medium heat. Cook and stir onion, garlic, and baby squash for about 5 minutes, until onions sweat and turn translucent. Stir in tomatoes and cook for about 1 minute more.

2. Turn off heat and mix in quinoa and salt and pepper to taste. Transfer to a bowl and stir in goat cheese. Spoon filling into the centers of the squash blossoms; slit blossoms open a bit if you are struggling with scooping it in cleanly. Place filled blossoms in skillet and warm over medium-low heat for about 5 minutes. Serve.

1 tablespoon extra-virgin olive oil
½ small red onion, diced
2 cloves garlic, finely minced
1 baby squash, diced
4 baby heirloom tomatoes, diced
1 cup quinoa, cooked
Salt and pepper to taste
¼ cup crumbled goat cheese
6 to 8 squash blossoms

Stuff squash blossoms with anything from crab salad to burrata, or even leftover hibiscus fried rice (page 92)— whatever you like.

Sunflowers

Botanical Name: *Helianthus annuus*

Nicknames: Ray flower

Language of Flowers: Sunflowers stand for loyalty and flexibility.

Background: In Greek myth, the water nymph Clytie was full of unrequited love for Apollo. She is said to have spent her days rooted to one spot, with her golden hair unbound and cascading over her shoulders, eating and drinking nothing except the morning dew so that she could watch the sun all day from when it rose in the east to when it set in the west. At last, her limbs did truly root to the ground and her face became the sunflower, which to this day continues to watch the sun.

The Latin name of the sunflower stands for flower (*anthos*) and sun (*helios*). It is widely believed by the Aztec and Inca peoples that the flower represents the sun, and it is worshipped accordingly. Here's the thing about a sunflower: not only does this pretty, cheery plant look impressive, it also has an interesting relationship to science and math.

Each sunflower is in fact a "composite flower" made of numerous florets all bunched together. The things that we refer to as "petals" are in fact the sterile florets, whereas the inner part, which we usually refer to as the "disk," contains the seed-bearing florets. Sunflower petals are far from randomly placed. They are almost without exception in an interconnecting spiral pattern (in math speak, a Fibonacci series).

Culinary Use: Sunflower petals taste grassy and slightly bitter; the unopened bud, however, tastes like steamed artichokes. Rich in nutrients, the flower seeds are considered a great food source and are turned into nut butters or eaten raw and toasted. Sunflower oil, pressed from the seed, is used for frying and in salads. The petals are also used in soups, salads, and beverages. The flower stalks, when young, can be peeled and eaten like celery.

Seasonality: Midsummer through fall, organic sunflowers can be grown in your garden or obtained at a farm stand.

Preparation: Do not eat the pollen! Sunflower pollen is a highly allergenic substance, so be sure to carefully wash your petals before cooking. Petals should be removed from the flower heads, and the white parts at the base of the flowers removed, because they are quite bitter.

Measure: 1 cup sunflower petals = petals from about 2 to 4 flowers.

Sunflower Bread

I love making bread. The air becomes perfumed with it, I experience the Pavlovian responses of mouth watering and stomach rumbling, and the whole room feels suddenly warm and homey. In this quick bread, sunflower petals and seeds, bittersweet and nutty, pair well with oats. I like to serve it in the morning, spread with a flower butter or cream cheese. *Makes one 9-by-5-inch loaf.*

1. Preheat oven to 450°F. Coat a 9-by-5-inch loaf pan with nonstick spray. Mix together 1 tablespoon each of the sunflower petals and sunflower seeds. Sprinkle mixture over the bottom of the pan, tilting the pan to get some of the mixture on the sides as well.

2. In a large bowl, combine oats, flour, baking powder, salt, the remaining 3 tablespoons sunflower petals, and 4 tablespoons of the sunflower seeds.

3. In a separate bowl, dissolve honey in vegetable oil. Stir in milk and yogurt. Combine honey mixture with flour mixture and stir to form a soft dough. Pour dough into the prepared pan and sprinkle the remaining 1 tablespoon sunflower seeds over top.

4. Bake bread for about 15 minutes. Reduce oven temperature to 300°F and bake bread for another 20 minutes, or until a toothpick inserted in the center of the loaf comes out clean. Let bread cool in the pan on a wire rack for 15 minutes before turning it out of the pan.

See page 178 for flower butter and cream cheese recipes.

¼ cup sunflower petals, divided
6 tablespoons sunflower seeds, divided
2 cups rolled oats
2 cups whole wheat flour
4 teaspoons baking powder
1 teaspoon salt
3 tablespoons honey*
2 tablespoons vegetable oil
1 cup milk
1 cup Greek yogurt

*I like to use strong-flavored local honey.

Steamed Sunflower Buds

My friend Laura's Italian mother, Mary, makes the best artichokes I've ever tasted. She is very indulgent and makes them for us often enough, but between artichoke fixes, when sunflowers are in season, I like to steam some sunflower buds and see if I can fool anyone into believing they are Mary's. The taste is surprisingly similar. *Serves 2.*

Pinch salt, plus more for seasoning
   and serving
6 sunflower buds
1 quart water or vegetable broth
4 sprigs parsley
6 garlic cloves
2 lemons, scrubbed and halved
¼ cup white wine
2 tablespoons extra-virgin olive oil
Freshly ground pepper to taste
Lemon juice, for serving

1. Bring a wide, deep pot of water to a boil over high heat and toss in a good pinch of salt. Peel and discard the tough, hairy green leaves from the bottom of the sunflowers. Cook buds for about 3 minutes. Drain buds in a colander.

   Partially cooking the buds in water removes a little of the bitterness.

2. In the same pot, stir to combine water or vegetable broth, parsley, garlic, lemon, wine, and oil. Bring to a simmer over medium heat. Add salt and pepper to taste. Return sunflower buds to pot, bottoms up. Cover and simmer for 20 to 30 minutes. Buds are done when you can poke the bottoms and feel no resistance. Drain buds and serve them with a sprinkle of lemon juice and a little salt.

Sunflower Chickpea Salad

Chickpeas are high in protein, low in fat, and substantial enough to be filling even when eaten in small amounts. This recipe is more of a guideline. Feel free to add whatever seasonal fresh vegetables and flowers are available in your garden or at the local farm stand. *Serves 4.*

1. In a large pot over medium heat, warm oil until it shimmers. Add onion, celery, carrot, and garlic. Add chickpeas and enough water to cover them by 2 inches. Add rosemary and thyme and bring to a boil. Reduce heat to low and simmer until chickpeas are fork-tender, about 1 hour. Drain chickpeas.

2. To make the dressing, whisk oil with lemon juice until mixture starts to form an opaque liquid. Add parsley, sunflower petals, red pepper, and garlic and whisk until oil and lemon juice come together and thicken.

3. Transfer chickpeas to a serving dish and drizzle dressing over top. If possible, I like to let the chickpeas marinate in the dressing for a good half hour before serving. This dish will last for 1 week in the refrigerator, and leftovers make a satisfying lunch.

CHICKPEA SALAD

1 tablespoon olive oil
1 onion, quartered
1 celery stalk, halved
1 carrot, halved
4 garlic cloves
1 pound chickpeas (aka garbanzos), soaked overnight and drained*
4 sprigs rosemary
4 sprigs thyme

SUNFLOWER DRESSING

1 tablespoon extra-virgin olive oil
1 tablespoon fresh lemon juice
1 tablespoon fresh parsley, chopped
1 tablespoon sunflower petals
⅛ teaspoon crushed red pepper
1 small garlic clove, minced

*You can substitute canned chickpeas, if necessary. Just skip step 1 and omit all other chickpea salad ingredients and go straight to the dressing.

Carrot Sunflower Sandwich Cookies

These treats, which have an earthy sweetness, are a real crowd-pleaser. The bittersweet sunflower goes so well with the carrot and a hint of brown sugar. They're delicious sandwiched with sweet, creamy sunflower cream cheese frosting. *Makes about 18 sandwiches.*

1. Preheat oven to 350°F. Line 2 baking sheets with parchment paper.

2. In the bowl of a food processor, process melted butter and sugars for about 1 minute. Add egg and yolk and process again.

3. Place carrots in a bowl. Add flour, oats, sunflower petals, baking powder, baking soda, salt, cinnamon, ginger, and nutmeg. Fold in butter mixture. Stir in optional mix-ins like pineapple, nuts, and raisins, if using. Refrigerate dough for at least 15 minutes.

4. Drop tablespoonfuls of cookie dough 2 inches apart on the prepared baking sheets. Bake for about 10 minutes, or until a toothpick inserted in the center comes out with just a few crumbs clinging to it. Let cookies cool on baking sheets until they reach room temperature.

5. Drop a dollop of frosting on half the cookies. Sandwich with the unfrosted cookies.

Try baking these cookies with various colors of sunflowers and carrots. Both grow in many glorious shades of yellow, orange, and red.

½ cup (1 stick) unsalted butter, melted
⅔ cup packed dark brown sugar
⅓ cup sugar
1 egg plus 1 yolk
1 cup grated carrots
1¾ cups all-purpose flour
¾ cup rolled oats
½ cup sunflower petals
1 teaspoon baking powder
½ teaspoon baking soda
¼ teaspoon salt
2 teaspoons cinnamon
1 teaspoon ginger
¼ teaspoon nutmeg
1 can crushed pineapple, drained (optional)
¾ cup walnuts (optional)
¾ cup raisins (optional)
2 cups sunflower frosting (page 183)

Tulips

Botanical Name: *Tulipa*

Nicknames: Lale

Language of Flowers: The color of the bloom indicates the meaning: variegated means beautiful eyes, red symbolizes irresistible love, and yellow signifies love with no hope of reconciliation.

Background: Most people think tulips originated in Holland, but they first grew as wildflowers in what is now Turkey, Syria, Iraq, and Iran. They were cultivated and sold across the globe by the Ottoman empire. Their name takes its origin from the Turkish word for turban, because of their distinctive shape. Persian legend says that tulips came forth from the blood and tears shed by a young lover who was stricken with unrequited love.

Culinary Use: Tulips taste of fresh lettuce and cucumber. They're best used as an edible vessel. But the petals work well in salads, and the bulbs make a good substitute for onions. The paler tulip petals are, the better they taste.

Seasonality: Tulips typically bloom from early to late spring. You'll want to eat tulips grown by you or a friend, for edible tulips are rarely available commercially. Florist tulips have most certainly been sprayed, unless they are sold by a certified organic grower.

Preparation: Simply remove the pistils and stamens and voilà, you have an edible bowl. Tulips and their petals can also lend flavor and beauty to salads, drinks, and appetizers. Grow some and surprise your friends.

Measure: 1 cup tulip petals = petals from about 3 to 7 flowers.

Tulip Martinis

I enjoy the flavor of vodka muddled with the subtle lettuce-cucumber taste of the tulip so much that I like to call this the Michetini. Arrogant? Maybe. But you'll see why. The lime and mint complement the tulip flavor, and the whole brings a sip of spring to your palate and your party. *Serves 6.*

Tear mint leaves in half and place in a deep bowl or glass pitcher. Add lime juice and tulip syrup. Muddle mint. Add tulip vodka and ice. Pour into glasses through a strainer and garnish with tulip petals.

12 mint leaves

¾ cup freshly squeezed lime juice

6 tablespoons tulip simple syrup (page 177)

1 generous cup tulip vodka (page 180)

1 cup ice

2 tulip petals, thinly sliced, or 6 tulip petals, used whole

Tulip Ice Cream Bowls

There are plenty of edible ice cream containers out there, but none so fetching as a tulip. A lovely tulip brimming with creamy ice cream is a sight to behold. I like to add a couple of fresh berries and a splash of tulip syrup. *Serves 4.*

Prop each tulip in a container that will help it stand upright, such as an eggcup or a champagne flute. Place 1 large scoop (or 3 small scoops) ice cream in each tulip. Drizzle a little tulip syrup over each and place a few fresh berries on the top. Serve immediately!

4 tulip blossoms, stamens and pistils
  removed
4 large or 12 small scoops ice cream
1 pint fresh berries
Several tablespoons tulip syrup
  (page 177)

Tulips make pretty edible bowls for ice creams, sorbets, and salads.

Spring Tulip and Pea Shoot Salad

Each year, I eagerly await my first from-the-garden meal. When the mint starts to unfurl, the pea shoots begin to shoot, and the chives lengthen, I hop outside to make a fresh spring salad. What better addition to this mix than some tulips? *Serves 2.*

Toss pea shoots, onions, mint, and tulip petals in a medium salad bowl. Sprinkle hazelnuts and feta on top. Combine lemon juice, mustard, salt, and pepper in a small bowl. Drizzle in oil while whisking continuously. Pour dressing over salad and toss gently to coat.

2 cups pea shoots
½ red onion, thinly sliced
¼ cup mint leaves, cut into long, thin strips
⅓ cup tulip petals, cut into long, thin strips
¼ cup hazelnuts, toasted*
¼ cup crumbled feta
2 tablespoons lemon juice
½ teaspoon mustard
¼ teaspoon sea salt
⅛ teaspoon freshly ground pepper
¼ cup hazelnut oil**

*Spread nuts on a baking sheet and toast them in a 350°F oven—tossing occasionally, for a consistent golden brown—for 8 minutes, or until they release a sweet nutty aroma.

**You may substitute almond or olive oil, but I like the distinctive taste of hazelnut oil.

For an easy method of quickly cutting petals and leaves, see "How to Chiffonade" (page 132).

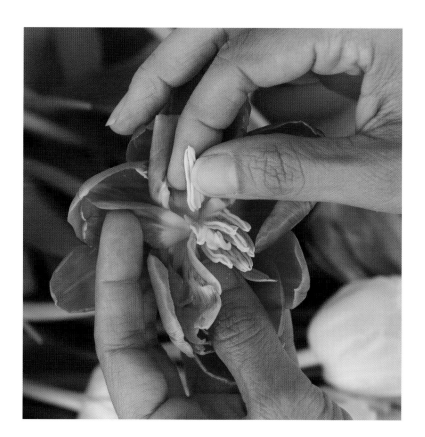

Violets

Botanical Name: *Viola*

Nicknames: Heartsease

Language of Flowers: Violets stand for modesty and faithfulness.

Background: The Greek word for violet is *io*. In ancient mythology, Io was the daughter of King Argos. Zeus fell in love with her but was concerned that his wife, Hera, would discover their illicit affair. So he turned Io into a cow and created sweet violets for her to feed upon.

Culinary Use: Herbal and sweet, violets are typically eaten whole or candied. They've graced kitchen tables since the 1300s, crowning desserts, flavoring jams and jellies, and adding color and whimsy to salads.

Seasonality: Violet leaves can be harvested almost all year long; the flowers bloom from earliest spring through early summer. They thrive in woodlands and spread themselves easily by runners (technically called stolons), which are horizontal stems that spread and connect plants. Unfortunately, violets are not commercially available—the blossoms can't be bought; they must be hunted. The plants grow in shady areas and are best plucked from a backyard that has not been chemically treated.

Preparation: Violets are ready to eat after a quick rinse and gentle pat dry. Pinch just beneath the flower to separate the blossoms from the plant.

Measure: 1 cup violets = about 50 to 70 flowers (used whole).

Violet Teacakes

These cookies are an adaptation of one of my grandmother's recipes. I am sure almost everyone has a similar family recipe filed away. My Bubbie called them Russian teacakes or, because of the shape she gave them, *hornchen* (meaning "little horn" in Yiddish), but they go by many names, such as *polvorones*, Mexican wedding cookies, Italian butter nuts, Swedish teacakes, and surely many more that I do not know. I took some liberties and turned these classic cookies into violet teacakes. I hope my Bubbie would approve. *Makes about 48 cookies.*

1. Preheat oven to 350°F. Line 2 baking sheets with parchment paper.

2. Beat butter, ½ cup of the confectioners' sugar, and violet syrup in a bowl with a mixer on medium high-speed for about 5 minutes. Add flour, salt, pecans, and violet petals and mix briefly, about 1 minute or less, until all the ingredients come together.

   At this point, you can freeze the dough in 1-inch balls until they are hard and then transfer them to a freezer bag and store them for up to 4 months.

3. Scoop 1-inch balls of dough and place them about 1 inch apart on the prepared baking sheets. Bake cookies for about 10 minutes, or until they have brown bottoms and are just beginning to turn golden brown everywhere else.

4. For the coating, pour the remaining 1 cup confectioners' sugar into a deep bowl of medium width. Mix in petal or luster dust, if using, until you have a color you like. (It is important to note that the color will darken on the cookie.)

5. Gently toss baked cookies in sugar coating one at a time until thoroughly coated. Transfer them to a plate to cool and develop their color. Eat these the same day, or store them in an airtight container for up to 5 days.

At Mali B, we make myriad variations of flower teacakes. For the Fourth of July, we do special red, white, and blue teacakes in rose, elderflower, and violet. To make your own variations, substitute another flower simple syrup for the violet and replace the coarsely chopped violet petals with those of another fresh flower.

1 cup (2 sticks) unsalted butter, room temperature
1½ cups confectioners' sugar, divided
1 tablespoon violet simple syrup (page 177)
2¼ cups all-purpose flour
¼ teaspoon salt
¾ cup pecans, finely chopped
2 tablespoons violet petals, coarsely chopped
Purple petal or luster dust, if desired*

*Petal and luster dusts are powders most often used to color sugar-paste flowers, but they can also add color and shine to desserts. They come in so many colors, you'll find that different brands have multiple variations on the same color. Feel free to mix and match until you find one you like. Find them at specialty baking shops and online (page 186).

Potato Salad with Violet Vinaigrette

This potato salad is almost not a recipe. Rather, it is something that is thrown together and looks and tastes fantastic. The real effort here goes into the jelly used to make the vinaigrette, but that recipe is so versatile that the work is worth it. *Serves 4.*

1. Fill a medium (4-quart) saucepan with water and add a pinch of salt. Bring to a boil, then reduce heat. Add potatoes and simmer until a fork pierces them easily. Drain.

2. Place potatoes and onion in a bowl and add enough oil to moisten them slightly. Drizzle salad with vinaigrette, a pinch of salt, and pepper to taste. Remember this is a taste thing, not an exact science.

2 pinches salt, divided
2 pounds new potatoes, cut into
    quarters
1 small red onion, diced small
Extra-virgin olive oil, to taste
Violet vinaigrette (page 182), to taste
Pinch freshly ground pepper

This salad can be served warm or cold, but if you chill it, taste it for seasoning before serving. It will taste a little different after the flavors have had a chance to mingle, and it might need more salt or pepper.

Violet Flower Cupcakes

Like tiny snowcapped mountains, these cupcakes capture your heart. They look delicate and airy but have the texture and crumb of a perfect pound cake, with a sweet violet jam surprise inside. *Makes 18 cupcakes.*

1. Preheat oven to 350°F. Line the wells of 18 muffin cups with cupcake liners.

2. In a bowl, whisk to combine flour, baking powder, and salt. Set aside.

3. Beat butter and sugar in another bowl with a mixer on medium-high speed for 5 minutes, until light and fluffy, scraping down the sides of the bowl as needed. Add vanilla and beat for 1 minute more.

4. Add egg whites to butter mixture one at a time, beating like crazy after each addition to lighten the batter and pausing to scrape down the sides of the bowl. This should take about 5 minutes in all.

5. Beat in flour mixture and coconut milk in alternating additions, starting and ending with flour mixture; do not overmix. Divide batter evenly among muffin cups. Bake for 25 minutes, or until a tester inserted in the center of a cupcake comes out clean. Let cool.

6. Place coconut flakes in a small bowl. Cut a cone-shaped piece of cake out of the top of each cooled cupcake and drop a dollop of violet jam into the well. Replace the caps on the cupcakes. Top each with a generous dollop of buttercream, and dip in coconut flakes. Top cupcakes with candied violets and serve.

Easy Homemade Cupcake Liners

For cups like the ones shown here, cut 6-inch squares of parchment paper. Turn a glass with a 2-inch diameter upside down. Place a parchment square on top and mold it by sliding your hands down and around the glass. Drop parchment cups into a cupcake pan and fill them with batter.

CUPCAKES

3 cups cake flour, sifted

1¼ teaspoons baking powder

1 teaspoon salt

1 cup (1 stick) unsalted butter, room temperature

2¼ cups sugar

1 teaspoon pure vanilla extract

4 egg whites

1 cup coconut milk (half of one 14-ounce can plus 2 teaspoons)

FROSTING AND TOPPING

⅓ cup violet jam (page 180)

3 cups violet buttercream (page 184)

1 cup unsweetened coconut flakes

About 24 candied violets (page 176)

Violet Macarons

Being Jewish, I grew up thinking that one ate macaroons once a year, that they came in a can, and that the only flavors they came in were almond or coconut or, once in a while, chocolate or chocolate chip. Imagine my confusion when, early in my college years, I took a trip to Paris and was presented with macarons. These were not even distant relatives of the confection I knew and grew up with. These were light and delicate, they came in a wide variety of flavors, and they were *pretty*. Now macarons are all the rage, and everyone should try to make them at least once. They are tricky but worth the effort. These violet macarons filled with violet buttercream couldn't be lovelier. *Makes about 24 cookies.*

1. Line three baking sheets with parchment paper and, if you are a real perfectionist (which I am not), draw 1½-inch-diameter circles about ½ inch apart on the parchment as a guide.

2. Process ground almonds and confectioners' sugar in the bowl of a food processor until mixture is completely blended and uniform.

3. Put egg whites in the bowl of a mixer fitted with the whisk attachment. Whip egg whites on high speed until they start to become foamy. Gradually add sugar over the course of a full minute. Beat on high speed for 5 minutes more, until thick and glossy.

4. Gently fold the almond mixture into the whipped egg whites, being ever so thorough and at the same time careful not to overwork the batter. Scoop batter into a pastry bag fitted with a round plain tip and pipe 1½-inch rounds of batter about ½ inch apart on prepared baking sheets. (For those of you who sketched circles in advance, this will be easy.)

    Use a rubber spatula to fold—don't stir!—the dry ingredients into the whipped egg whites without deflating them. It is tricky to get this part right, but it should be easy once you get the hang of it.

5. If using candied violets, place one on each of half of the circles. Let them sit at room temperature for 1 hour before baking so circles can begin to develop

1⅔ cups confectioners' sugar
1⅓ cups finely ground blanched almonds*
3 egg whites**
2 tablespoons sugar
About 24 candied violets (page 176), optional
1 cup violet buttercream (page 184)

* To make your own, grind whole blanched almonds to a fine powder in a food processor.

** Aged egg whites are preferable; they're easier to whip than fresh egg whites.

a little crust. This is how macaron shells get their "feet," their signature ruffled base.

6. Preheat oven to 275°F. Bake shells for about 20 minutes, or until they develop feet and start to get crispy on top. Let them rest at room temperature for another 30 minutes or so to stabilize. At this point, you can fill them or stack them carefully in an airtight container and freeze for up to 1 month.

7. To fill macarons, load violet buttercream into a pastry bag fitted with a round plain tip. Pipe a small dollop on each of the plain shells and top them with the shells that have violet flowers on top. Once macarons are filled, eat within the day.

Violet Crème Caramels

The combination of custard and caramel is something of a wonder: A few simple ingredients come together to create a silky-smooth velvety texture. Most crème caramel is served turned over so the caramel is on top, but I like to serve mine in teacups or jelly jars, with the caramel as a treat when you get to the bottom. Either way, the addition of violets makes this version special. *Makes 6 servings.*

½ cup sugar
2½ cups milk
1 vanilla bean, split and scraped
1 cup violet sugar (page 176)
3 eggs plus 3 egg yolks*

*Use leftover egg whites to make violet macarons (page 172) or other treats. Store them in plastic zip-top bags in the freezer or refrigerator; write the date and the number of egg whites clearly on the bag.

1. Preheat oven to 350°F. Place 6 oven-safe teacups, ramekins, or jelly jars into a baking pan large enough to accommodate them (a 9-by-13-inch pan should do).

2. Cook sugar with 2 tablespoons water in a small saucepan over medium heat, stirring constantly, for about 3 minutes, until sugar is fully melted and golden brown. Pour equal amounts of melted sugar into each of the 6 cups.

3. Bring milk and vanilla scrapings (discard the bean) to a fast simmer in a saucepan over medium heat; meanwhile, whisk violet sugar with eggs and egg yolks in a large bowl or a 4-cup measuring cup until thoroughly combined. Pour in a little hot milk, stirring constantly; keep pouring and stirring until hot milk is fully incorporated and mixture is smooth and creamy. Divide cream evenly among the cups.

   It's important to whisk the milk into the egg mixture slowly to prevent the eggs from curdling.

4. Pour about 2 inches of water into the pan the cups are in, either before or after you move the pan to the oven. (I like to set my pan on the pulled-out oven rack and then pour in the water.)

5. Bake for about 30 minutes, or until custard has lost most of its jiggle. Remove cups from the water and let them come to room temperature. Refrigerate for a few hours before serving.

The Basics: Simple Recipes for Stocking Up

The tried-and-true recipes that follow work for most any edible flower—roses, lilacs, dandelions, herb flowers, you name it. Not only that, they store well and can be used in most any recipe. Preserve the blossoms in sugars, oils, vinegars, vodkas, butters, and soft cheeses; they'll last into the winter, and they'll infuse everything with lovely floral flavor and color. By stocking up on these basics while your favorite edible flowers are in bloom, you'll be able to fill your kitchen with blossoms all year long.

Dried Flowers

Most flowers dry well and can be used in teas and syrups, which can in turn be enjoyed on their own or used to infuse sweet and savory dishes year round. To substitute dried flowers for fresh, you will need only one-third of the amount of the flower; for example, if a recipe calls for 1 cup of fresh rose petals, you will need only 1/3 cup of dried rose petals.

To dry flowers, place a brown paper bag on a baking sheet and cover it with paper towels. Arrange a single layer of clean flowers on top, spaced about 1/4 inch apart. Place the baking sheet in a warm, dry spot for at least 2 days—perhaps a bit longer for larger flowers. Store dried flowers in an airtight container in a cool, dark place. They will gradually lose their color but retain their flavor; they are best used within 1 year. The notable exception is lavender, which holds its scent for many years.

Flower Sugars

During the height of flower season, I find myself hoarding all the canning jars just to store my flower sugars. This way I can use them in winter for a taste of summer. You'll love the different colors and scents that the sugars take on over time.

In a clean jar, layer about 1/2 cup flowers per 1 cup sugar and let the scent infuse over time. (Lavender requires much less: just 2 table-spoons per 1 cup sugar will do.) If the sugar absorbs enough moisture that it starts to clump, a short spin in the food processor will revive it. Flower sugars have an incredibly long shelf life. I have had success with flower sugars up to one full year after making them.

For especially vibrant, flavorful flower sugars, grind sugar with flowers in a food processor for 2 minutes, or until pulverized, before storing in jars.

Candied Flowers

Candied flowers are well-preserved gems that last long enough to be used all year.

2 cups sugar*
1 egg white, whisked until foamy
About 25 large (or 50 small) flowers,
    such as violets, violas, pansies, roses,
    or rose petals

*This is one of those times when it is useful to use refined (regular granulated) white sugar. You simply will not achieve the same results with organic sugar.

Line a baking sheet with parchment paper. Pulse sugar in a food processor until superfine and powdery. With a small, clean paintbrush, brush the petals of each flower gently but thoroughly with egg white. Sprinkle with sugar to coat, shaking off excess. Place on the prepared baking sheet and let dry for at least 10 hours and up to overnight. Store in a single layer in an airtight container for up to 1 year.

Flower Simple Syrups

Colorful flower-infused simple syrups have oh so many uses. Strong and sweet, they are best used as bases in other recipes, such as sorbets or drink mixes.

2 cups sugar

1 cup water

2 tablespoons to 1 cup fresh or dried flowers*

*The following variations specify amounts of fresh flowers. If using dried blooms, use one-third the amount called for.

Dissolve sugar in water over medium heat, stirring occasionally, until it reaches a simmer. Place flowers in a nonreactive bowl (by that I mean glass, enamel, or stainless steel). Pour hot syrup over top and let stand for at least 30 minutes. Strain the mixture and discard the flowers. (I know it is a shame to discard the flowers, but you must unless you are using the syrup right away.) Floral simple syrup can be stored in the fridge for 1 or 2 months. If it begins to crystallize, simply heat it again until smooth. *Makes 2 cups (1 pint).*

This recipe makes a viscous simple syrup. For a thinner version, use 1 cup sugar and 1 cup water. Either type will work well in recipes that call for simple syrup.

Borage Basil Simple Syrup: Use 1/4 cup borage flowers and 1/4 cup basil leaves and/or basil flowers.

Elderflower Simple Syrup: Use 1/2 cup elderflowers (6 or 7 flowers) and add the juice and zest of half a lemon along with them.

Herbal Simple Syrups: Use 1/2 cup herb leaves, 3/4 to 1 cup herb flowers, or 3/4 cup mixed herbs and herb flowers.

Lavender Simple Syrup: Use only 2 tablespoons lavender buds. Lavender is a potent herb, and this syrup will get stronger the longer you let it infuse, so be careful to taste for your own preferences.

Lime-Scented Geranium Simple Syrup: Use 1 cup lime geranium petals and/or 1/2 cup leaves. (Use more geranium leaves for a stronger scent and flavor; the petals are less potent.) Other scented geraniums work well too.

Rose Simple Syrup: Use 1 cup rose petals.

Tulip Simple Syrup: Use the petals of 2 tulips (about 1 cup).

Violet Simple Syrup: Use 1 1/2 cups violets.

Flower Syrups

These flower syrups are similar to flower simple syrups but much thinner and easier to pour, perfect for using as a finishing syrup over pancakes, waffles, or ice cream.

2 to 3 cups fresh or dried flower blossoms

2 cups boiling water

1/2 cup sugar

1/4 to 1 cup fresh or frozen fruit (optional)

Flower syrups and simple syrups vary in color from golden to amber to deep blue.

Place blossoms in a medium bowl and pour boiling water over them. Let stand for at least 2 hours and up to 24 hours. In a small saucepan over medium heat, bring flower water, sugar, and fruit (if using) to a simmer. Cook for 4 minutes. Remove from heat and pour through a fine mesh strainer into a glass container. Discard the solids. Refrigerate for up to 1 month. *Makes 2 cups (1 pint).*

Borage Basil Syrup: Use 2 cups borage blossoms and 1/4 cup basil leaves instead of fruit.

Chamomile Peach Syrup: Use 2 cups chamomile and 1 cup chopped peaches.

Dandelion Apricot Syrup: Use 2 cups dandelion petals and 1 cup chopped apricots.

Lavender Blueberry Syrup: Use 1/4 cup lavender buds and 1/4 cup blueberries.

Lilac Blackberry Syrup: Use 2 cups water, 3 cups lilac blossoms (stems removed), $1/2$ cup sugar, and 4 tablespoons fresh or frozen blackberries. Bring berries to a simmer, along with the sugar and water, and cook and stir mixture for 4 minutes. Strain and discard berries along with the flower solids.

Rose Raspberry Syrup: Use 3 cups rose petals and $1/4$ cup raspberries.

Flower Rock Candy

Here's a fun use for flower simple syrup. Dip candy sticks or 8-inch pieces of string in flower simple syrup and then roll them around in plain sugar or flower sugar. Place on a parchment-lined baking sheet and let dry overnight. The next day, warm flower simple syrup in a saucepan over medium heat and add sugar $1/4$ cup at a time, waiting until it completely dissolves before adding more. (The total amount of sugar you need will depend on the humidity, the mineral content of your water, and the flower you use.) When the

liquid stops absorbing sugar, pour it into a clean, heatproof container that's at least 8 inches wide and 6 inches deep. Suspend the sugar-coated sticks in the liquid. Move your project to a dark place and leave it alone for about 2 weeks. When the sticks are loaded with sugar crystals, suspend them briefly over a clean container to dry.

Make flower-powered rock candy jewelry! Imagine little flower girls walking down the aisle in glittering sugar necklaces, or women going to cocktail parties with a sugar bauble hanging from their necks or perched on their fingers.

Flower Rock Candy Jewelry: Use clean ribbon or embroidery thread. Instead of dangling one end into the liquid, loop it in so crystals will form in a wide arc (for necklaces or bracelets) or a narrow one (for rings). Tape ribbon to the sides of the jar if necessary to hold in place.

Flower Butters and Flower Cheeses

The simplest way to use flowers—aside from tossing them in a salad—is by making a compound butter or cheese. Use flower butters in savory dishes to add nice subtle flower flavors with ease. (I love sautéing freshly caught fish in nasturtium butter or putting a little rose butter on top of steak.) Delight guests with an array of flower butters on your breakfast table or flower-fortified cheeses on your cheese plate.

To 1 (8-ounce) package, or 1 cup of any soft, room-temperature butter or cheese, add $1/4$ cup to 1 cup flowers, $1/2$ teaspoon salt, $1/4$ teaspoon pepper, and any other desired seasonings. Stir to incorporate. Cover and refrigerate butters for up to 2 weeks or freeze for up to 6 months; soft flower cheeses should be consumed within 1 week.

Calendula Butter or Cheese: Use $1/2$ cup calendula petals per 2 cups (1 pound) butter or cheese.

Dandelion Butter or Cheese: Use ¼ cup dandelion petals per 2 cups (1 pound) butter or cheese.

Herb Flower Butter or Cheese: Use ⅓ cup chive florets or mixed herb flowers per 2 cups (1 pound) butter or cheese.

Lavender Butter or Cheese: Use up to 2 tablespoons lavender buds per 2 cups (1 pound) butter or cheese.

Nasturtium Butter or Cheese: Use 1 cup nasturtiums per 2 cups (1 pound) butter or cheese.

Pansy Butter or Cheese: Use ¼ cup pansies or violas per 2 cups (1 pound) butter or cheese.

Rose Petal Butter or Cheese: Use ½ cup rose petals. Add ½ teaspoon rose water (optional) per 2 cups (1 pound) butter or cheese.

Flower-Glazed Cheeses

Either at dinner's end or its beginning is a good time to serve beautiful flower-glazed cheeses. The flowers in a glazed cheese don't add as much to the flavor as they would if they were folded in, but they make a stunning presentation.

1 cup dry and drinkable white wine
1 (¼-ounce) package gelatin (about 2½ teaspoons)
3 or 4 flowers, such as pansies, herb flowers, or rose petals
1 wedge brie, or any cheese without a rind or with an edible rind

Pour wine into a small saucepan, add gelatin, and let it absorb for about 5 minutes. Cook and stir over medium heat for 2 to 3 minutes, until gelatin is fully dissolved. Remove from heat and let it cool slightly (but don't let the gelatin set). Set a wire rack over a baking sheet, put cheese on the rack, and arrange flowers on top. Brush the wine mixture lightly over top. Put the rack in the refrigerator for 10 minutes, until the gelatin is firm. Brush the flowers with the wine mixture a few more times before serving to ensure the flowers are fully covered.

If you are glazing cheeses with dark flowers (like these purple pansies), the color will begin to bleed within 4 to 6 hours. So make sure you don't wait that long before serving.

Flower Jams

The epitome of summer in a jar, flower jams capture the essence of the blossom. Though the amounts of ingredients differ slightly, the method remains the same.

¼ to 2 cups flower petals
2 to 3 cups water
1 to 4 tablespoons lemon or lime juice
1½ to 4 cups sugar
1 (3-ounce) packet powdered pectin

Place blossoms in a sealable heatproof jar and pour boiling water over top. Let stand for at least 2 hours and up to overnight; you want a strong infusion for jam, and the longer it steeps, the stronger it gets. Strain the mixture and press all the liquid you can out of the blossoms; discard or leave them in if desired. In a 3- to 4-quart nonreactive pot (stainless steel or enamel, not aluminum), bring the flower-infused water, lemon or lime juice, and sugar to a boil. When sugar is dissolved, add pectin and return to a full rolling boil for 3 minutes. Skim off any foam that develops on the surface, because it will affect the taste and appearance of your jam (especially if you use organic sugar). Ladle jam into clean, dry jars. Can or refrigerate. Canned jams will last for at least 1 year; refrigerated jams will last for a couple months. *Makes 4 (8-ounce) jars.*

Dandelion Jam: Use 2 cups dandelion petals, 3 cups water, 1 tablespoon lemon juice, 2¼ cups sugar, and 1 (3-ounce) packet powdered gelatin.

Dianthus Jam: Use 1 cup dianthus petals (white bits removed), 2 cups water, 1 tablespoon lemon juice, 1½ cups sugar, and 1 (3-ounce) packet powdered pectin.

Elderflower Jam: Use 1 cup elderflowers, 3 cups water, 2 tablespoons lemon juice, 3 cups sugar, and 1 (3-ounce) packet powdered pectin.

Hibiscus Jam: Use ½ cup hibiscus, 2 cups water, 4 tablespoons lemon juice, juice from ½-inch piece fresh ginger, 4 cups sugar, and 1 (3-ounce) packet powdered pectin.

Lavender Jam: Use 4 tablespoons lavender, 3 cups water, ¼ cup lemon or lime juice, 4 cups sugar, and 1 (3-ounce) packet powdered pectin.

Lilac Jam: Use 2 cups lilacs, ¼ cup lemon or lime juice, 3½ cups sugar, and 1 (3-ounce) packet powdered pectin.

Nasturtium Jam: Use 1½ cups nasturtiums, 2 cups water, ¼ cup lemon juice (or a dash of hot sauce, like Tabasco), 2 cups sugar, and 1 (3-ounce) packet powdered pectin.

Rose Jam: Use 2 cups roses, 3 cups water, 2 tablespoons lemon juice, 2 cups sugar, and 1 (3-ounce) packet powdered pectin.

Violet Jam: Use 2 cups violet jam, ¼ cup lemon juice, 4 cups sugar, and 1 (3-ounce) packet powdered pectin.

I'd been canning fruit preserves for years before I actually tried preserving flowers. My first flower jam project was adding pineapple sage flowers to my apricot jam, and it was amazing. The recipes here are for exclusively flower jams, but please, by all means, try your hand at adding flowers to fruit jellies and jams. Just be sure to strain out the flowers before you do the final canning.

Flower Vodkas

A flower-infused vodka is a fairly simple thing. Place chopped or whole flowers—a mixture or all one kind—in a jar with a lid. Cover with vodka, cap the jar, refrigerate for at least 1 week, and voilà, flower vodka. When it tastes good enough to drink, strain it and rebottle it in a clean jar. Store in the fridge or freezer.

The flowers listed here are especially good in vodka, and lavender tastes just as great infused in gin!

Borage Vodka: Use 1 cup borage flowers per 2 cups vodka.

Dianthus Vodka: Use 1 cup dianthus per 1 cups vodka.

Elderflower Vodka: Use ½ cup elderflowers per 2 cups vodka.

Lavender Vodka: Use 2 tablespoons lavender buds per 2 cups vodka.

Nasturtium Vodka: Use ½ cup nasturtium flowers per 2 cups vodka.

Tulip Vodka: Use 1 cup tulips per 2 cups vodka.

Flower Ice Bowls and Ice Cubes

Pretty flower ice bowls look great on your table and are useful for holding drinks, fruits, ice creams, or anything else you want kept cold. Ice cubes are a brilliant way to drop flowers into your drinks.

Flower Ice Bowls: Choose 2 freezer-proof glass or stainless-steel bowls of different sizes that will nest well. Place flowers in the bottom of the larger bowl and cover with ½ inch of water; flowers will likely float to the top, which is fine. Nest the smaller bowl inside the larger one. Use a piece of tape to keep it centered, if necessary. Freeze for 1 hour, or until ice forms almost all the way through. Add a thin layer of water and a few more flowers to the larger bowl, and refreeze. Continue to add flowers and water a little at a time, ending with a final addition of water to cover the flowers. (Tip: If you're in a rush, brush a tiny bit of butter onto one side of the flowers so they stick to the outside of the larger bowl and won't move when you fill the bowl with water.) To unmold, run the outside of the larger bowl under cold water, and the ice bowl will pop right out. You can line the inside with edible leaves (such as geranium, hosta, or lettuce) to protect your food from absorbing too much water as the ice melts.

Flower ice bowls are the perfect serving vessel for fruit salad or shrimp cocktail. Extra-large ice bowls make great holders to chill champagne or a pitcher of your favorite beverage. Single-serving ice bowls are a lovely way to serve sorbet or ice cream.

Flower Ice Cubes: Place a flower in the bottom of each mold and fill trays half full of water; flowers will likely float to the top, which is fine. Freeze for 1 hour, and then fill the trays with more water and freeze again to encase the flowers in ice. I like to make flower cubes by the dozens and keep them in plastic zip-top bags in the freezer for when I have friends over.

Flower Wines

Any mix of flowers and fruit makes for a delicious cordial (a homespun liqueur) that is commonly called country wine. Cleanliness is key, since flower wines and cordials ferment at room temperature. Make sure your kitchen counters, hands, and utensils are sterile, and thoroughly wash and dry all ingredients.

Place 4 cups flowers in a large heatproof container. Pour 6 cups boiling water over top. Cover and let steep for at least 4 hours and up to 24 hours. Pour the resulting tea through a fine-mesh strainer into a large pot or saucepan, pressing the petals to extract as much flavor as possible. Discard blossoms and bring tea to a boil. Place 2½ cups sugar in a heatproof 1-gallon jar. Pour boiling flower tea into the jar and stir to dissolve sugar. Add 1 to 2 sliced citrus fruits. Cover jar and let liquid stand for 2 weeks at room temperature, shaking every couple days. Pour flower wine through a fine-mesh strainer lined with a coffee filter into a clean container. Serve or cover and store, refrigerated, for up to 3 weeks.

Sterilize your jars and tools by immersing them in boiling water. Or you can wash them in an oxygen-based cleaner (such as OxiClean), which won't leave a film like most detergents. When a sterile environment is especially important—as when brewing flower wine—you can use a biodegradable, environmentally friendly sanitizer with a low pH, such as Star San, to wipe everything down. Available from home-brew supply stores, safe sanitizer makes things easy because it doesn't affect taste and is OK to ingest in small amounts.

Some of the flowers that make lovely flower wines include pinks (dianthus), lilac, lavender, daylily, elderflower, violet, tulip, herb flowers, roses, and pansies. Swap in equal amounts of whatever flowers you like, except for lavender; because it has a particularly strong flavor, lavender should always be used in smaller amounts.

Flower Teas

Making flower tea is a method of extracting flower material—technically called a decoction—and infusing water with the essence of the flower. Use flower tea in place of water in most any recipe, and you'll enrich it with flower flavor.

I use flower teas in recipes for caramels, jams, and marshmallows. You may find yourself experimenting with it in lots of your favorite dishes. Think about using vibrant orange calendula tea to boil your pasta for mac and cheese, perhaps!

Place 1 tablespoon fresh (or 1 teaspoon dried) flowers in a cup. Pour 1 cup boiling water over top and steep for 5 minutes. Strain out the petals before drinking or using in a recipe.

Chamomile flower tea, dandelion blossom tea, elderflower tea, or hibiscus tea, they're all made with this ratio of flowers to boiling water. Again, the exception is lavender tea, which is best made with 1 teaspoon lavender flowers (or 1/3 teaspoon dried lavender flowers) per 1 cup boiling water.

Iced Flower Teas: Make these a gallon at a time. Just use 4 cups flowers to 1 gallon boiling water. Store in the fridge after simmering and straining the brewed tea.

Flower Vinegars

Because they are infused with color and flavor and can be stored indefinitely in the fridge, flower vinegars are extremely useful. Put blossoms in a jar that has a tight-fitting lid. Warm vinegar in a saucepan over low heat for 4 or 5 minutes. Pour it over the flowers. Cap the jar and leave it where it can capture sunlight for 1 week. Move it to a cool, dry place or the refrigerator, and let it sit for 1 week more. Strain out the blossoms, and store flower vinegar in a clean, capped jar in the refrigerator.

Chive Blossom Vinegar: Use 2 cups chive blossoms and 1½ cups white wine vinegar.

Four Thieves Vinegar: Use 1 tablespoon each lavender, rosemary, mint, sage, and thyme leaves and/or flowers, 2 crushed garlic cloves, and 2 cups white wine vinegar.

Nasturtium Vinegar: Use 2 cups nasturtium flowers and/or leaves and 2 cups white wine vinegar.

Rose Petal Vinegar: Use 2 cups rose petals and 2 cups white wine vinegar.

Flower Vinaigrettes

Using flower vinegars or flower jams to make better-than-basic vinaigrettes is a breeze. Combine flower vinegars with shallots, mustard, salt pepper, and extra-virgin olive oil.

Combine flower jams with extra-virgin olive oil and vinegar. Whisk for about 2 minutes (or shake in a lidded jar) until the vinaigrette comes together. *Makes about 3/4 cup.*

Chive Blossom Vinaigrette: Use 2 finely chopped shallots, 1 teaspoon Dijon mustard, 2 tablespoons chive blossom vinegar, 1¼ teaspoons salt, 1/4 teaspoon ground pepper, and 6 tablespoons extra-virgin olive oil.

Nasturtium Vinaigrette: Follow recipe for chive blossom vinaigrette, but swap nasturtium vinegar for the chive blossom vinegar.

Rose Petal Vinaigrette: Follow recipe for chive blossom vinaigrette, but swap rose vinegar for the chive blossom vinegar.

Violet Vinaigrette: Use 3 tablespoons violet jelly, 2 tablespoons extra-virgin olive oil, and 1 tablespoon white wine vinegar. Add 1 teaspoon Dijon mustard and a pinch of salt or pepper if desired.

Flower Whipped Creams

Just think how a lightly scented flower whipped cream will dress up your party. Put some on a slice of pie, a dish of ice cream, a pile of fresh berries, or a shortcake, and instantly you have dressed up your dessert.

2 cups very cold heavy cream
1 tablespoon to 1 cup flower petals
   (or 2 teaspoons to 2 tablespoons
   flower simple syrup)
½ teaspoon pure vanilla extract*
¼ cup confectioners' sugar

*Omit if using flower simple syrup.

Put heavy cream, flower petals (or flower syrup), vanilla, and confectioners' sugar in a large mixing bowl. Chill for at least 30 minutes and up to overnight. Strain out the petals. With a mixer fitted with the whisk attachment, whip the mixture on high speed for 3 minutes, or until it forms soft, billowy peaks. Serve right away or refrigerate for up to 4 hours. Makes 4 cups (1 quart).

Basil Whipped Cream: Use 1 cup basil flowers or 2 tablespoons basil simple syrup.

Dianthus Whipped Cream: Use 1 cup dianthus flowers or 2 tablespoons dianthus simple syrup.

Elderflower Whipped Cream: Use 1½ tablespoons elderflower simple syrup (because elderflowers shouldn't be eaten raw).

Hibiscus Whipped Cream: Use 1 cup hibiscus flowers or 2 tablespoons hibiscus simple syrup.

Lavender Whipped Cream: Use only 1 tablespoon lavender buds or 2 teaspoons lavender simple syrup.

Rose Petal Whipped Cream: Use 2 cups rose petals or 1½ tablespoons rose petal simple syrup.

Scented Geranium Whipped Cream: Use ⅓ cup scented geranium flowers or, for a richer geranium flavor and aroma, use a mix of scented geranium flowers and leaves; geranium leaves are edible and more potent than the flowers. Or you can use 1 tablespoon scented geranium simple syrup.

Flower Pastry Creams

Infused with flowers, pastry creams have so many uses—layering cakes, filling doughnuts, topping pies, and more. *Mise en place* is important when making this delicate treat, so have all your ingredients measured and ready to use before you start.

1 cup milk
1 cup heavy cream
½ to 1 cup flower sugar, divided
Pinch salt
6 egg yolks
2 tablespoons cornstarch
4 tablespoons butter
1½ teaspoons pure vanilla extract

Warm milk and cream in a medium saucepan over medium-low heat. Stir in all but 2 tablespoons of the sugar. Keep your eye on the milk mixture, whisking occasionally to dissolve the sugar and prevent the mixture from boiling. Whisk to combine egg yolks and the remaining 2 tablespoons sugar in a nonreactive heatproof bowl (stainless steel or enamel, not aluminum). Slowly whisk half the milk mixture into the egg mixture. Then whisk the milk–egg mixture back into the saucepan. Increase heat to medium, add cornstarch, and whisk until the cream starts to cling to your whisk and threatens to bubble. Remove from heat and whisk in butter and vanilla. Transfer the pastry cream to a bowl. Cover it with plastic wrap touching the surface of the cream to prevent a skin from forming. Refrigerate for at least 2 hours before using. *Makes 3 cups.*

Hibiscus Pastry Cream: Use ½ cup hibiscus sugar.

Hollyhock Pastry Cream: Use ½ cup hollyhock sugar.

Lilac Pastry Cream: Use 1 cup lilac sugar. Add a pinch of cardamom along with the vanilla.

Scented Geranium Pastry Cream: Use 1/2 cup scented geranium sugar.

Light and Fluffy Flower Cream: Whip 1 cup cold heavy cream to soft peaks and then gently fold flower pastry cream into it.

Flower Frostings

Try using cream-cheese-based flower frostings for everything from dressing up vanilla cupcakes to quickly topping fresh cinnamon rolls. I like to sandwich it between two carrot sunflower cookies (page 159). You can make a double or triple batch of frosting and freeze the extra in an airtight plastic container for up to 6 months.

1 (8-ounce) package cream cheese
1 cup confectioners' sugar, sifted, plus more to taste
2 tablespoons milk
1 teaspoon pure vanilla extract
1/3 to 1 cup flower petals

Put all the ingredients in the bowl of a mixer. Beat slowly at first, to let the confectioners' sugar start to absorb,

and then increase speed to medium-high; beat for 3 to 4 minutes until no lumps remain. Taste and beat in more confectioners' sugar, if desired. Note that overbeating will cause the frosting to lose its stiffness. *Makes 3 cups.*

Any edible flower—or a mix—works in this frosting recipe. I love to have calendula, dandelion, rose petal, sunflower, and viola frostings on hand.

Flower Buttercream Frostings

At Mali B, the only buttercream we ever use is a variation on a Swiss meringue buttercream. It is smooth, creamy, and light. With a little flower simple syrup and a few fresh blossoms, you can transform this buttercream into a floral beauty.

1/4 cup water
1/2 cup sugar, divided
3 egg whites
1 tablespoon flower simple syrup
1/4 to 1/2 cup flowers (optional)
1 cup (2 sticks) unsalted butter, room temperature, cut in 1-tablespoon pieces

Bring water and 1/4 cup of the sugar to a boil in a small saucepan. Boil until the temperature reaches 240°F on a candy thermometer; meanwhile, put egg whites in a bowl. When the temperature reaches 240°F, beat whites with a mixer fitted with the whisk attachment on high speed for 1 minute, until the whites start to get foamy. Gradually beat in the

remaining 1/4 cup sugar. Reduce the mixer speed to low and slowly and carefully pour in the boiling sugar syrup. Beat on high speed for 8 to 10 minutes, or until the bottom of the mixer bowl is room temperature again. Return mixer speed to low and add flower simple syrup. Beat in butter a few pieces at a time. Beat frosting on high speed for about 30 seconds, until butter is fully incorporated. Use immediately or refrigerate in an airtight container for up to 1 week. *Makes 2 cups.*

Lilac, rose, hibiscus, calendula, dandelion, and violet buttercreams are among my favorites.

Flower Ice Creams

Wonderfully creamy, with a subtle floral flavor, this flower ice cream is great on its own but works equally well melting over a tart or cobbler or topping a cool bowl of fruit or a slice of pound cake.

2 cups heavy cream
2 cups milk
1/2 cup sugar

¼ to ½ cup flower petals

4 egg yolks

Zest and juice of 1 lime or other citrus fruit

¼ to ⅓ cup flower simple syrup

Warm cream and milk in a saucepan over medium heat until the liquid comes to a bare simmer. Stir in sugar and flower petals and simmer, stirring, until the sugar dissolves. In a medium bowl, use a fork to combine yolks with lime juice. Gradually whisk about half the steamy milk mixture into yolk mixture. Then slowly whisk the yolk-milk mixture back into the saucepan. Cook and stir until it thickens and the temperature reaches about 165°F on a candy thermometer. Stir in flower simple syrup. Strain the mixture through a fine-mesh strainer into a 1-quart container. Refrigerate for at least 6 hours. (I like to chill it overnight to make sure it's really cold.) Process ice cream in an ice-cream maker according to manufacturer's instructions. *Makes 1 quart.*

Elderflower Ice Cream: Use ½ cup elderflowers and ⅓ cup elderflower simple syrup.

Lavender Honey Ice Cream: Reduce sugar to ¼ cup and use ¼ cup fresh lavender (or 3 tablespoons dried). Add ½ cup honey along with the flowers to the cream, milk, and sugar. Omit lime juice and simple syrup.

Rose Petal Ice Cream: Substitute 2 tablespoons rose water for the lime juice. Use ¼ cup rose simple syrup and add ¼ cup chopped rose petals (optional) just before processing.

Flower Sorbets

Since they're made with flower-infused water (basically, a flower tea), sorbets can be made with fresh or dried flowers. There's nothing like a fantastic flower sorbet in January or February to help beat those winter blues.

2 cups water

¼ cup sugar

2 tablespoons lime juice or other citrus juice

2 cups fresh or dried flowers*

*Use any flower but lavender, which is better in ice cream (the cream softens lavender's potent flavor).

Bring water, sugar, and citrus juice to a boil. Pour the mixture over flowers, and let it steep for at least 10 minutes and up to 24 hours before straining out and discarding petals. Chill for at least 2 hours. Process the chilled mixture in an ice-cream maker according to manufacturer's directions. Store in the freezer for up to 3 months. For the best flavor, let sorbet sit at room temperature for about 15 minutes before serving. *Makes 1 quart.*

Herb flower sorbet is particularly delicious. So are elderflower, hibiscus, lilac, pansy, rose, and violet sorbets.

Flower Lemonades

It's hard to go wrong with fresh flower simple syrups and citrus. This recipe is a basic guideline. Mix and match with flower vodkas for refreshing happy hour concoctions.

1 cup flower simple syrup

4 to 5 cups water or sparkling water

1 cup lemon juice or ¾ cup lime juice

Mix ingredients directly in the pitcher. Adjust the flavors to your own taste preferences.

If you're using juice in place of water, reduce the amount of flower simple syrup by half.

Hibiscus Basil Watermelonade: Use ½ cup hibiscus simple syrup, ¼ cup basil simple syrup, and 5 cups watermelon juice.

Lilac Lemonade: Use 1 cup lilac simple syrup, 1 cup lemon juice, and 4 cups water.

Sparkling Geranium Limeade: Use 1 cup lime-scented geranium simple syrup, 5 cups sparkling water, and ¾ cup lime juice.

Summer parties will never be dull when you give cocktails a floral twist. Lavender lemonade goes well with a touch of gin, and hibiscus basil watermelonade mixes well with champagne.

Sources

Seeds and Starter Plants
Diane's Daylilies (dianedaylilies.com)
Johnny's Selected Seeds (johnnyseeds.com)
Peaceful Valley Farm Supply (groworganic.com)
Renee's Garden (reneesgarden.com)

Fresh-Cut and Dried Flowers
Koppert Cress (koppertcress.com)
Frontier Natural Products Co-op (frontiercoop.com)
Marx Foods (marxfoods.com)
Melissa's (melissas.com)
Starwest Botanicals (starwest-botanicals.com)

Always measure flowers loosely packed in measuring cups—be gentle, and don't worry about being too precise.

Specialty Tools and Ingredients
Bees Needs Honey (newyorkmouth.com)
Bob's Red Mill (bobsredmill.com)
Crate and Barrel (crateandbarrel.com)
Global Sugar Art (globalsugarart.com)
JB Prince (jbprince.com)
King Arthur Flour Company Bakers Catalog
    (kingarthurflour.com)
Pfeil & Holing (cakedeco.com)
Sugar Craft (sugarcraft.com)
Sur La Table (surlatable.com)
Target (target.com)
Valrhona (valrhona.com)
Williams-Sonoma (williams-sonoma.com)
Young Living Essential Oils (youngliving.com)

Metric Conversion Chart

Volume

American	Imperial	Metric
1 tsp		5 ml
1 tbsp		15 ml
½ cup (8 tbsp)	4 fl oz	118 ml
1 cup (16 tbsp)	8 fl oz	237 ml
1 pint (2 cups)	16 fl oz	473 ml

Weights

American	Metric
1 oz	28 g
4 oz (¼ lb)	113 g
8 oz (½ lb)	227 g
12 oz (¾ lb)	340 g
16 oz (1 lb)	454 g

Oven Temperatures

	°F	°C	Gas Mark
Very cool	250–275	130–140	½–2
Cool	300	148	2
Warm	325	163	3
Medium	350	177	4
Medium hot	375–400	190–204	5–6

Acknowledgments

Thank you seems hardly enough for all the support I received while working on this book, but it is my utmost pleasure to say it! So, THANK YOU:

To Laura Chamaret for seeing "something" and letting me show it. To Margaret McGuire for going beyond editor and into the realm of "book whisperer." To Katie Hatz, Jane Morley, Mary Ellen Wilson, Nicole De Jackmo, Eric Smith, and the rest of the team at Quirk Books. To my dear friend, "spiritual and menu advisor," and "not lawyer" Josh Goldstein for helping me look both ways before crossing the street and for always believing in me. To Eagle, Holly Guzman, Donna Light, Leila Carney, Micheal Tierra, and Christopher Hobbs for nurturing my knowledge of plants and the medicine they make. To Matt Michel from Rolling In Dough Pizza for experimenting with me and tasting more "interesting" foods than he can remember. To the staff at Mali B, notably Hannah RB Smith, Isabelle Torgove, Ida Mollica, Amelia Harsh Rallis, Brittany Calderale, Isaiah Aqui, Jordan Bacher, and Ijie Bacher for rolling with it, for keeping customers happy, for never saying no when I throw a new recipe at you, and for seeing the joy in it. To Lizz Salaway for having faith. To Allie at Marx Foods and Nico at Koppert Cress for supplying flowers that always look and taste their best. To Ron Apostle and Oysterponds Farms, Mary Woltz from Bees Needs Honey, Karen and Fred at Sang Lee Farms, Karen at Catapano Dairy Farm, Wickams fruit farm, and my friend Megan Barron, for providing us with some of the most beautiful ingredients on earth. To Claire Bean for loving flowers as much as I do and for bringing me all sorts of beauties at a moment's notice. To Ken Ludacer and Ginger McFadden from Beall & Bell, Robby Beaver and the Frisky Oyster, Noah Schwartz and Noah's, and Linda Kessler and Kessie's Korner for their generosity with space and props. (If ever you are in Greenport, find them.) To Susan Ringo for her fabulous cornbread. To Lori Catalano and Anthony LaSala for tirelessly working to help make sure our photo shoots were working fun, for patiently waiting while every food and flower had its time in the light, and for selflessly tasting every morsel. To Miana Jun whose work is exceptional and without whose enthusiasm and attention to detail this book would not be nearly as sensual! To Laura McCarthy whose love and generosity could fill the pages of a thousand books; your home and heart are so open and I am lucky. To my sister Stacey and my sister-in-law Holly for listening and paying attention, for believing in me, and for always helping before ever being asked. To my parents Sara Ruth and Dick, my stepfather Bob, and my in-laws Jason and Iris for being great teachers of life. To Nanao for being one of the best people I know, for making every day fun even when it is not, for sharing laughs and a sense of humor, for inspiring me and indulging me in my desire to try all new things, and for being the best collaborator in the history of collaborators. To Jordan and Ijie for being the best sons a mother could ask for. I hope you are as proud of me as I am of you. You are my reasons. And to Noah for being my fact checker and sounding board, for cheerleading and championing, and for being uncompromisingly and unfailingly supportive, and most of all, for looking at me through the lens of love.

To my readers: I hope you'll enjoy cooking with flowers as much as I do. Work hard, but take time to eat your roses.

—Miche Bacher

Index

light and fluffy flower cream, 183
lilac blackberry syrup, 104, 178
lilac jam, 109, 180
lilac lemonade, 185
lilac pastry cream, 107, 183
lilac pavlova with lime sorbet and
    lilac berry syrup, 104
lilac sorbet, 106
lime-scented geranium simple
    syrup, 177
lime sorbet, 104
lilac sugar, 104, 176

mango buttercream, 81
mango orchid sticky rice, 124
measuring flowers, 9

nasturtium butter or cheese, 179
nasturtium jam, 117, 180
nasturtium pizza, 115
nasturtium tea sandwiches, 132
nasturtium thumbprint cookies, 117
nasturtium vinaigrette, 182
nasturtium vinegar, 182
nasturtium vodka, 180

orchid pineapple upside-down
    cake, 125
orchid seafood sauté, 121

oven-baked doughnuts with lilac
    cream filling, 107

pansy butter or cheese, 179
pansy lollipops, 131
pansy petal pancakes, 130
pansy rhubarb galettes, 135
pansy simple syrup, 130, 135, 177
pansy sugar, 135, 176
pansy tea sandwiches, 132
passionfruit orchid tartlets, 126
picking flowers, 8
pickled pink petals, 45
pineapple sage and ham tea
    sandwiches, 132
pineapple sage biscotti, 83
pink rosé wine cake, 51
pink tuiles, 48
pistachio rose shortbread, 140
poor man's asparagus, 40
popcorn–chive blossom
    cupcakes, 78
potato salad with violet
    vinaigrette, 169
preparing flowers, 10, 22, 34, 42,
    52, 62, 70, 90, 102, 112, 118,
    128, 136, 144, 152, 160, 166

roasted daylily buds, 40
rose jam, 180
rosemary flower madeleines, 89
rosemary flower margaritas, 88

rosemary simple syrup, 88, 138, 177
rose petal biscotti, 83
rose petal butter or cheese, 179
rose petal ice cream, 185
rose petal vinaigrette, 182
rose petal vinegar, 182
rose petal whipped cream, 143, 183
rose-scented geranium filo cups, 67
rose-scented geranium whipped
    cream, 67, 183
rose raspberry syrup, 178
rose simple syrup, 177

salads, 37, 114, 120, 157, 165, 169
sandwiches, 132
scented geranium pastry cream,
    67, 183
scented geranium whipped cream,
    67, 183
sorbets, 104, 106, 185
sparkling geranium lemonade, 185
spring tulip and pea shoot salad, 165
squash blossom quesadillas, 149
squash blossom tempura, 147
steamed sunflower buds, 156
storing flowers, 8
stuffed squash blossoms, 150
sunflower bread, 154
sunflower chickpea salad, 157
sunflower frosting, 159, 183
sweet William shortbread, 46

Thai orchid and beef salad, 120
tulip ice cream bowls, 163
tulip martinis, 162
tulip simple syrup, 162, 177
tulip syrup, 163, 177
tulip vodka, 162, 180

violet buttercream, 171, 172, 184
violet crème caramels, 175
violet flower cupcakes, 171
violet jam, 171, 180
violet macarons, 172
violet simple syrup, 168, 177
violet sugar, 175, 176
violet teacakes, 168
violet vinaigrette, 169, 182

washing flowers, 8
white pepper thumbprint cookies
    with lilac jam, 109

Want to learn more about *Cooking with Flowers?*

Visit Quirkbooks.com/CookingWithFlowers:

✤ Find exclusive recipes that we couldn't fit into the book

✤ Discover bonus recipes for the medicinal and cosmetic use of flowers:
  salves, oils, and teas for healing

✤ Download recipe cards

✤ Read a Q&A with author Miche Bacher

✤ Join in the conversation

About the Author

Miche Bacher cofounded Mali B Sweets with Nanao Anton in the waterfront village of Greenport, New York. Mali B's cakes, chocolates, shortbreads, and other small indulgences are made with fresh local ingredients—and plenty of flowers—and are available in the studio, by special order, or from the online shop. Mali B's confections have been lauded by *Food Network Magazine*, *Hamptons* magazine, *HC&G*, *WellWed*, *Brides New York*, and the *New York Times*. Their hand-painted peony cake was named one of the 24 most beautiful cakes in America by *Brides* magazine.

Though Miche has loved flowers all her life—and spent many happy hours as a girl making dandelion jewelry and lilac mud pies in her grandparents' garden—her real knowledge of flowers didn't begin until the late 1980s. She and her future husband, Noah, moved into a "cottage" (read plywood shack) on a vast property that had once been a commune. It had woods, gardens, and water. But for Miche, the selling point was the bathtub; it was set amongst the blackberry brambles in the flower garden. It was on that property that she became a life-long gardener and had her first taste of edible flowers, starting with potluck salads of baby greens studded with the spicy flavor of brilliant orange nasturtiums. Soon Miche fell headlong into the study of herbal medicine, earning an acupuncture degree and gaining an appreciation for flowers as food and medicine for the body as well as the spirit.

Miche has worked alongside some of the world's most renowned chefs and is dedicated to bringing excellence and innovation to the table. She is constantly seeking out creative uses for herbs, flowers, and spices in recipes both savory and sweet. Miche resides in Greenport with her husband and fact-checker, Noah, her sons, Jordan and Elijah, and their dog, Mali.